The D

Anne Parrish, Dillwyn Parrish

Alpha Editions

This edition published in 2021

ISBN : 9789355343086

Design and Setting By
Alpha Editions
www.alphaedis.com
Email - info@alphaedis.com

THE DREAM COACH

If you have been unhappy all the day,
Wait patiently until the night:
When in the sky the gentle stars are bright
The Dream Coach comes to carry you away.

Great Coach, great Coach, how fat and bright your sides,
To please the child who rides!
Painted with funny men—see that one's hose,

How blue! How red and long is that one's nose!

And under this one's arm a flapping cock!

Great dandelions tell us what o'clock

With silver globe much bigger than the moon——

Dream Coach, come soon! Come soon!

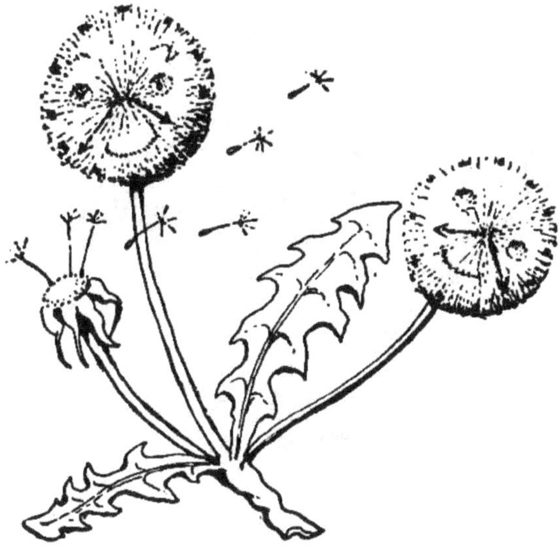

What pretty pictures! Angels at their play,
And brown and lilac butterflies, and spray
Of stars, and animals from far away,
Grey elephants, a bright pink water bird;
Things lovely and absurd.

As the wheels turn, they wake to lovely sound,
Musical boxes—as the wheels go round
They play a little silver spray of notes:
"Swift Runs the River"—"Bluebells in the Wood"——
"The Waterfall"—"The Child Who Has Been Good"——
Like splash of foam at keel of little boats.

Under a sky of duck-egg green
Have you not seen
The hundred misty horses that delight
To draw the coach all night,
And the queer little Driver sitting high,
And singing to the sky?

His hat is as tall as a cypress tree,
His hair is as white as snow;
His cheeks and his nose are as red as can be;
He sings: "Come along! Come along with me!"
Let us go! Let us go!
His coat is speckledy red and black,
His boots are as green as a beetle's back,
His beard has a fringe of silver bells
And scarlet berries and small white shells,
And as through the night the Dream Coach gleams,
The song he sings like a banner streams:

"Nothing is real in all the world,
Nothing is real but dreams."

Through sound of rain the Dream Coach gallops fast.
All those that we have loved are riding there:
I hear their laughter on the misty air.
I wait for you—I have been waiting long:
Far off I hear the Driver's tiny song——
Oh, Dream Coach! Come at last!
(From *Knee-High to a Grasshopper.*)

The Seven White Dreams of the King's Little Daughter

When the Driver of the Dream Coach reached the last small star in the sky, he unharnessed his hundred misty horses and put them out to pasture in the great blue meadow of Heaven. It was well he reached the end of his journey when he did, for in another moment a mounting wave of sunlight and wind, rushing up from the world far below, blew out the silver-white flame of the star so that no one could follow the strange Driver and his strange Coach to their resting place.

Resting place? What a mistake! The Driver of the Dream Coach never rests. You see, there are so many things to do even when he is carrying no passengers. There are new dreams to invent: queer dreams, funny dreams, fairy dreams, goblin dreams, happy dreams, exciting dreams, short dreams, long dreams, brightly colored dreams, and dreams made out of shadows and mist that vanish as soon as one opens one's eyes. Then there is the very bothersome matter of keeping the records straight, records of those who deserve good dreams, those who need cheering with ridiculous dreams, and those, alas, who have been bad and naughty and have to be punished (how the little Driver hates this!) with nightmares. It is hard to keep all those dreams from getting mixed up, there are so many of them. Indeed, sometimes, they do get mixed up, and a good child, who was meant to have a dream as pretty as a pansy or as funny as a frog, gets a nightmare by mistake. But the Driver of the Dream Coach tries as hard as he possibly can never to let this happen. He has so very much to do that he never would catch up with his work no matter how quickly his beautiful horses galloped from star to star, from world to world, if there was not some one to help him.

There are little angels who help the Driver of the Dream Coach.

In their gold and white book they keep a record of every one on earth.

As soon as the Driver of the Dream Coach had unharnessed his horses he went to these angels and planned his next trip. What a busy night it was to be! If I should use all the paper and all the pencils in the world I could not begin to tell you about all the dreams he arranged to carry to the sleeping world.

And yet there was one child who was nearly forgotten, a little Princess whose name had been written at the top of a new page which the Driver had neglected to turn in his hurry.

"Surely you are not going to forget the little Princess on her birthday!" pleaded the little angels, turning the page.

"Oh, dear!" said the Driver. "That will never do; now, will it? And yet—I simply can't pack another dream into the Coach. I'm sorry, but I'm afraid——"

"Oh, dear!" echoed the angels.

"Perhaps——"

Just then one of the youngest angels, who happened to be leaning over the parapet of Paradise, saw the Princess begin to cry, and took in the situation instantly. So he hurried to the others and suggested that he himself should carry a dream to the little Princess.

The Driver of the Dream Coach thought this was a splendid idea and thanked him again and again for his help.

That is how the seven white dreams of the King's little daughter were carried to her by an angel, and as you know (or if you don't, I will tell you) the dreams carried in the moonbeam basket of the angels are the most beautiful of all.

What did the Princess dream?

That you shall hear.

I cannot remember all the names of the King's little daughter, and indeed few can. The Archbishop who christened her says that he can, but he is so great and so deaf a dignitary that no one would think of asking him to prove it. They are all there, twelve pages of them, in the great book where are recorded the baptisms of all the Royal babies, so that you can look for yourself if none of the ones I can remember—Angelica Mary Delphine Violet Candida Pamelia Petronella Victoire Veronica Monica Anastasia Yvonne—happen to please you.

It was the fifth birthday of the little Princess, and there were to be great celebrations in her honor. Fireworks would blossom in the night sky, and in the gardens lanterns were hung like bubbles of colored light from white rose tree to red, while the great fountains would turn from pink to mauve, from mauve to azure, to amber, and to green, as they flung up slender stems and great spreading lacy fronds of water. Every one from the King down to the smallest kitchen-maid had new clothes for the occasion, and the Chief Cook had created a birthday cake iced with fairy grottoes and gardens of spun sugar, so huge and so heavy that the Princess's ten pages in their new sky-blue and silver liveries, staggered under the weight of it.

The little Princess had a new gown of white satin, sewn so thickly with pearls that it was perfectly stiff, and stood as well without her as when she was inside it. It was standing by her bedside when the bells of the city awoke her on her birthday morning, together with her silver bath shaped like a great shell, and her nine lace petticoats, and her hoops to go over the petticoats, and her little white slippers on a cushion of cloth-of-silver, and her whalebone stays, and her cobweb stockings, and her ten Ladies-In-Waiting, Grand Duchesses every one. When she opened her blue eyes they all swept her the deepest curtsies, their skirts of bright brocade billowing up about them, and said together:

"Long Life and Happiness to Your Serene Highness!" and then the first Grand Duchess popped her out of bed and into her bath, where she got a great deal of soap in the Princess's eyes while she conversed in a most respectful and edifying manner.

The second Grand Duchess, who was Lady-In-Waiting-In-Charge-Of-The-Imperial-Towel, was even more respectful, and nearly rubbed the Princess's tiny button of a nose entirely off her face.

The third Grand Duchess brushed and combed the little duck tails of yellow silk that covered the Royal head; and *oh*, how she did pull!

The fourth Grand Duchess was Lady-In-Waiting-In-Charge-Of-The-Imperial-Shift, and as she was rather old and slow, although extremely noble, the Princess grew cold indeed before the shift covered up her little pink body.

The fifth Grand Duchess put on the rigid stays.

The sixth put on the stockings and slippers.

The seventh was very important and gave herself airs, for the nine lace petticoats were her concern.

The eighth Grand Duchess was Lady-In-Waiting-In-Charge-Of-The-Imperial-Hoops.

The ninth put on the little Princess the dress of satin and pearls, that glowed softly like moonlit drops of water.

And the tenth Grand Duchess, the oldest and ugliest and noblest and crossest and most respectful of them all, placed on the yellow head the little frosty crown of diamonds.

Then the Princess's Father Confessor, a very noble Prince of the Church, dressed in violet from top to toe, came in between two little boys in lace, and said a long prayer in Latin. It was so long that, I am sorry to have to tell you, right in the middle the Princess yawned, so of course another long prayer had to be said to ask Heaven to overlook such shocking wickedness on the part of Her Highness.

Then the Chief-Steward-In-Attendance-On-The-Princess brought her breakfast—bread and milk in a silver porringer. The little Princess had hoped for strawberries, as it was her birthday, but the Chief Gardener was saving every strawberry in the Royal gardens for the great Birthday Banquet that was to be held that evening.

Then the little Princess went to say good morning to her Mother and Father, and this is the way she went.

First came two heralds in forest green, blowing on silver trumpets. Then came the Father Confessor and his little lace-covered boys. Then came the Ladies-In-Waiting in their bright brocades, with feathers in their powdered hair, and after each lady came a little black page to carry her handkerchief on a satin cushion. The ten pages of the Princess were next, and after them came the Royal Baby's Own Regiment of Dragoons in white and scarlet. And last came four gigantic blacks wearing white loin cloths and enormous turbans of flamingo pink, and carrying a great canopy of cloth-of-silver fringed with pearls, and under this, very tiny, and looking, in her spreading gown, like a little white hollyhock out for a walk, came the Princess.

The nine lace petticoats were her concern.

After she had curtsied, and kissed the hands of her Royal parents, her Father gave her a rope of milk-white pearls and her Mother gave her a ruby as big as a pigeon's egg, both of which were instantly locked up in the Royal treasury. They then bestowed upon her, in addition to her other titles, that of Grand Duchess of Pinchpinchowitz, which took so long to do that when she had said thank you it was time for lunch, which was just the same as breakfast, except that this time the porringer was gold.

After lunch the Prime Minister read the Princess an illuminated Birthday Greeting from her loyal subjects, which ran along so that the Ladies-In-Waiting nearly yawned their heads off behind their painted fans, and the Princess had a nice little nap, and dreamed that there would be strawberries for supper.

But instead there was bread and milk in a porringer covered with turquoises and moonstones.

Then, as the younger Ladies-In-Waiting were thinking of the Gentlemen-Of-The-Court who would be waiting for them among the rose trees and yew hedges, to watch the colored water of the fountains and listen to the harps and flutes, and as the older Ladies-In-Waiting were thinking of comfortable seats out of a draught in the State Ball Room, and having the choicest morsels of roasted peacock and larks' tongue pie and frozen nectarines, they popped the Princess into bed pretty promptly—indeed, an hour earlier than usual—and went off to celebrate her birthday.

The room in which the little Princess lay was as big as a church, and the great bed was as big as a chapel. Four carved posts as tall as palm trees in a tropic jungle, held a canopy of needlework where hunters rode and hounds gave chase and deer fled through dark forests. Below this lay the broad smooth expanse of silken sheet and counterpane, and in the midst, as little and alone as a bird in an empty sky, lay the King's little daughter.

One large tear rolled down her round pink cheek, and then another. The long dull day had tired her, and the great dim room frightened her, and she wanted to see the fireworks she had heard her pages whispering about. She sat up among her lace pillows, and her tears went splash, splash, on the embroidered flowers and leaves of her coverlet.

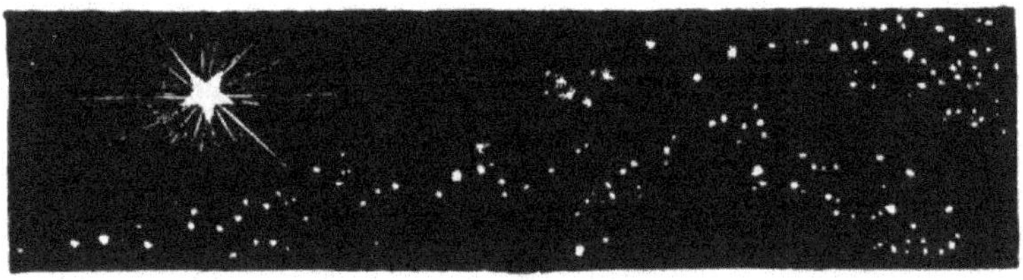

One of the youngest angels happened to be leaning over the parapet of Paradise when the Princess began to cry, and he took in the situation instantly, and hurried off to his Heavenly playmates to tell them about it. "It is her birthday," he said, "and no one has given her as much as a red apple or a white rose—only silly old rubies and pearls that she wasn't even allowed to play marbles with! And now they have left her to weep in the dark while they dance and feast! I shall go down to her and sit by her bed till her tears are dry, and take her a white dream as a gift."

"Oh, let me send a dream too!" cried another angel. "And let me!" "And let me!" So that by the time the little angel was ready to start to earth there were seven white dreams to be taken as birthday gifts from Heaven, and he had to weave a basket of moonbeams to carry them in.

That night the Princess dreamed that she was a daisy in a field, dancing delicately in the wind among other daisies as thick as the stars in the Milky Way. Feathery grasses danced with them, and yellow butterflies danced above, and the larks in the sky flung down cascades of lovely notes that scattered like spray on the joyous wind.

Some poor little girls were playing in the field. Their feet were bare and their faded frocks were torn, but they danced and sang too. There came a rumbling like thunder, and through a gap in the hawthorn hedge the children and the daisies saw the King's little daughter driven past in her great scarlet coach drawn by eight dappled horses. They could see the little Princess sitting up very straight with her crinoline puffing about her and her crown on her head, and after she had passed all the children played that they were princesses, making daisy crowns for their heads, and hoops of brier boughs to hold out their limp little petticoats.

The next day the Princess looked in vain for a daisy as she took her morning constitutional in the Royal gardens. There were roses and lilies, blue irises, and striped red and yellow carnations tied to stakes, all stiff and straight.

"Hold up your head, Serene Highness!" snapped one of the Ladies-In-Waiting, who had had too many cherry tarts at too late an hour the night before.

But daisies danced in the Princess's heart.

The next night the Princess dreamed that she was a little white cloud afloat in the bright blue sky. She floated over the blue sea and the white sand, and over black forests of whispering pines, and over a land where fields of tulips bloomed for miles, in squares of lovely colors, delicate rose and mauve and purple, coppery pink and creamy yellow, with canals running through them like strips of old, dark looking-glass. She floated over rye fields turning silver in the wind, and over nuns at work in their walled gardens, and finally over a great grim palace where a King's little daughter lived. "I would rather be free and afloat in the sky," thought the small white cloud.

When she took the air the next day, she looked up to see if any white clouds were in the sky. "Her Highness is growing very proud," said the Ladies-In-Waiting. "She holds her nose up in the air as a King's daughter should."

On the third night, the Princess dreamed she was a little lamb skipping and nibbling the new green grass in a meadow where hundreds of lilies of the valley were in bloom. They were still wet and sparkling with rain, but now the sun shone and a beautiful rainbow arched above the meadow and the lilies of the valley and the happy little lamb.

Through the rest of her life the gentleness of the lamb lay in the heart of the Princess.

The next night she dreamed that she was a white butterfly drifting with other butterflies among the tree ferns and orchids of the jungle, gentle and safe from harm, although serpents lay among the branches of the trees and lions and tigers roamed through the green shadows.

A white butterfly flew in at her window the next day. "A moth! A moth!" cried the Ladies-In-Waiting. "Camphor and boughs of cedar must be procured instantly, or the dreadful creature will eat up Her Highness's ermine robes!"

But the little Princess knew better than that.

On the fifth night she dreamed that she was a tiny white egg lying in a nest that a humming bird had hung to a spray of fern by a rope of twisted spider's web. The nest was softly and warmly lined with silky down, and above her was the soft warmth of the mother bird's breast.

On the sixth night she was a snowflake. It was Christmas night, and the towns and villages were gay. Rosy light poured from every window, blurred by the falling snow, and the air was full of the sound of bells. High up on the mountain was a lonely wayside shrine with carved and painted wooden figures of the Mother and Her Child whose Birthday it was. There were no bells there, nor yellow candle light, but only snow and dark evergreen trees. The snowflake, whirling and dancing down from the sky, a tiny frosty star, gave its life as a birthday gift to the Holy Child, lying for its little moment in His outstretched hand.

The angel was distressed to find, on the seventh night, that the seventh dream had slipped through a hole in the moonbeam basket and was lost. Careless little angel! But it really did not matter, for instead of a dream, he showed himself to the Princess. And she liked that the best of all, for she had never had any one to play with before, and there is no playmate equal to an angel. But the seventh dream is still drifting about the world—I wonder where? Perhaps it will be upon my pillow to-night—perhaps upon yours. Who knows?

Goran's Dream

Crack! went the Driver's whip, but it did not hurt the galloping misty horses, for it was only a ribbon of rainbow that he liked to use because both he and his horses thought it so pretty. And away went the great Coach, over the forests and over the seas, over the cities and plains, to a country where the sea thrusts long silver fingers into the land, where mountains are white with snow at the same time that the meadows are bright with wild flowers, and where in summer the sun never sets, and in winter it never rises. And here the Dream Coach drew up beside a cottage where a lonely little Norwegian boy was falling asleep.

"Come, Goran!" called the Driver. "Come, climb into the Coach and find the dream I have brought for you!"

Who was Goran? What dream did he find?

That you shall hear.

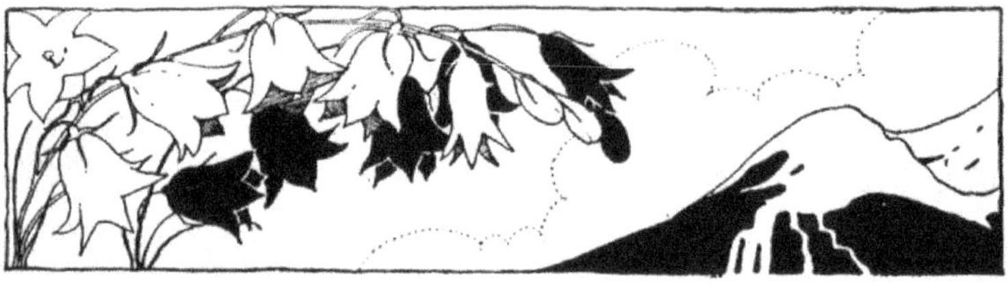

Little Goran and his grandmother lived in a tiny house in Norway, high above the deep waters of a fjord. When Goran was a baby they used to tie one end of a rope around his waist and the other to the door, so that if he toddled over the edge he could be hauled back like a fish on a line. But now he was no longer a baby, but a big boy, six years old, and he tried to take care of his grandmother as a big boy should.

It was a lovely spot in summer, when the waterfalls went pouring down milk-white into the green fjord, sending up so much spray that they looked as if they were steaming hot; when rainbows hung in the sky; when the small steep meadows were bright with wild flowers, and even the sod roof of the cottage was like a little wild garden of harebells and pansies and strawberries that Goran gathered for breakfast sometimes. He was happy all day then, fishing in the fjord, making a little cart for Nanna, the goat, to pull, trying to teach Gustava, the hen, to sing, putting on his fingers the pink and purple hats that he picked from the tall spires of wild foxglove and monkshood, and making them dance and bow, and listening to the loud music of the waterfalls after rain.

And in the evening after supper Goran's grandmother would tell him splendid stories while they sat together in the doorway making straw beehives, sewing the rounds of straw together with split blackberry briers. The sun would shine on the straw and make it look so yellow and glistening that Goran would pretend he was making a golden beehive for the Queen Bee's palace. For where Goran lived the sun never sets at all in the middle of summer, and it is bright daylight not only all day, but all night as well. You and I would never have known when to go to bed, but Goran and his grandmother were used to it, and even Gustava, the hen, knew enough to put her head under her wing and make her own dark night.

But with winter, changes came. The flowers slept under the earth until spring's call should wake them, and yawning and stretching, *s-t-r-e-t-c-h-i-n-g*, they should stretch up into the air and sunlight. The waterfalls no longer flung up clouds of spray like smoke, but built roofs of ice over themselves. And, strangest of all, the winter darkness came, so that the days were like the nights, and you and I would never have known when to get up.

"I must go to the village for our winter supplies before the snow falls and cuts us off," his grandmother said to Goran one day. "Neighbor Skylstad has offered me a seat in his rowboat to-morrow, and will bring me back the next day. You won't be afraid to stay here alone, will you, Goran?"

"No, Grandmother," said Goran. He pretended to be tremendously interested in poking his finger into the earth in a geranium pot, so that his grandmother shouldn't see that his eyes were full of tears and his lower lip was trembling. For to tell you the truth he was frightened. The little house was so far from any other house, and then Goran had never spent a night alone. Last year when the winter's supplies were bought, he had gone to the village with his grandfather, and he had told Nanna and Gustava and Mejau, the cat, all about what a wonderful place it was, a thousand times over; the warm shop, with its great cheeses in wooden boxes painted with bright birds and flowers, and its glowing stove, as tall and slim as a proud lady in a black dress, with a wreath of iron ferns upon her head; the other children who had let him play with them while grandfather exchanged the socks and mittens knitted by grandmother for potatoes and candles. And they had slept at the inn under a feather bed so heavy that you would have thought by morning they would have been pressed as flat as the flowers in grandmother's big Bible. But they weren't! They got up just as round as ever, and had a wonderful breakfast of dark grayish-brown goats'-milk cheese, cold herring, and stewed bilberries. Grandfather had gone to

Heaven since then, and Goran wondered if he could possibly be finding it as delightful as the village.

How he did want to go this time! But of course he knew that some one must stay behind to feed Nanna and Gustava and Mejau, to tend the fire and water the geraniums and wind the clock. So he said as bravely as he could: "I'll take care of everything, Grandmother."

Soon after his grandmother left, the snow began to fall. How that frightened Goran! Suppose it snowed so hard that she could never get back to him! For when winter really began, the little house was often up to its chimney in snow, and they could get to no one, and no one could get to them.

How poor little Goran's heart began to hammer at the thought! He fell to work to make himself forget the snow. First, seizing a broom made of a bundle of twigs, he swept the hard earth floor, which in summer had so pretty a carpet of green leaves, strewn fresh every day by Goran and his grandmother. Then he poured some water on the geraniums in the window, only spilling a little on himself. Then he stroked Mejau, who was purring loudly in front of the fire; and all this made him feel much better.

"Time for dinner, Goran!" said the old clock on the wall. At least it said:

"Ding! Ding! Ding! Ding! Ding! Ding! Ding! Ding! Ding! Ding! Ding! Ding!" which meant the same thing.

So Goran ate the goats'-milk cheese and black bread that his grandmother had left for him; and then, and not before, he summoned up enough courage to look out to see if the snow was still falling.

It was snowing harder than ever, and already everything had a deep fluffy covering. Oh, would his grandmother ever be able to get back to him? But he must be brave, and not cry, for he was six years old. He said a little prayer, as his grandmother had taught him to do whenever he was frightened or unhappy, and his heavy heart grew lighter.

"I'll make a snowman," Goran decided. Perhaps then the time would seem shorter. Grandfather and he had made a splendid snowman after the first snowfall last winter.

It was not late enough in the year to have the day as dark as night. It was only as dark as a deep winter twilight, and the white snow seemed to give out a light of its own for Goran to work by.

First he found an old broomstick and thrust it into the snow so that it stood upright. Then he pushed the heavy wet snow around it, patting on here, scooping out there, until there was a body to hold the big snowball he rolled for the head. A bent twig pressed in made a pleasant smile, and for eyes Goran ran indoors and took from the little box that held his treasures two marbles of sky-blue glass that his grandfather had given him once for his birthday.

What a beautiful snowman! With his sky-blue eyes he gazed through the falling snow at little Goran.

"Ding! Ding! Ding! Ding! Ding!" called the old clock, and that was the same as saying:

"Time for supper, Goran!"

The fire lit up the room with a warm glow, painted the curtains crimson, and made wavering gigantic shadows on the walls. The water bubbled in the pot, and the boiling potatoes knocked against the lid. "Prr-prrr!" said Mejau, blinking in front of the blaze, and the old clock answered:

"Tock! Tick! Tock!"

Goran had given their supper to Nanna and Gustava and Mejau, and had taken one good-night look at his snowman. Now he put his bowl of boiled potatoes on the table in front of the fire, and pulled up his chair.

Lying on the floor where she had fallen from his box when he was getting his snowman's blue eyes was a playing card, the Queen of Clubs. His grandfather had found it lying in the road in the village, and had brought it home as a present for Goran. The little boy thought the Queen was very splendid, with her crown and her veil, and her red dress trimmed with bands of blue and leaves and stars and rising suns of yellow. In one hand she held on high a little yellow flower. Now he picked her up and put her on a chair beside him, pretending the Queen had come for supper to keep him from being lonely. Each mouthful of potato he first offered her, with great politeness, but the delicate lady only gazed off into space.

Goran's supper made his insides feel as if a soft blanket had been tucked cozily about them, and he was warm and sleepy.

"Was there anything else Grandmother told me to do before I went to bed?" he murmured.

"Tick! Tock! Yes, there was," the Clock replied. "She told you to wind me up. Climb on a chair and do it carefully. Don't shake me. I can't stand that, for I'm not as young as I used to be."

"And I want a drink!" cried the youngest geranium, who was little, and had been hidden by the bigger pots when Goran watered them.

Knock, knock, knock!

What a knocking at the door! Goran ran to open it, and the firelight fell on Nanna the Goat and Gustava the Hen against a background of whirling snow. Nanna was wearing Grandmother's quilted jacket—where in the world had she found that? And Gustava had wrapped Goran's muffler about herself and the little basket she carried on her wing.

"Good evening!" began Nanna, rather timidly for her. "May Gustava and I come in and sit by the fire? We thought you might be lonely, and then it is so cold in the shed. I did have a muffler like Gustava's, but I absent-mindedly ate it. I'm growing *very* absent-minded. We've come with an important message for you, but I can't remember what it is. Can you, Gustava?"

"Cluck! Clu-uck! No, I can't. But I've brought my beautiful child to call on you," said Gustava; and she lifted her wing and showed Goran the brown egg in her basket.

"Shut the door! Shut the door!" several Geraniums called indignantly. "We are very delicate, and we shall catch our deaths of cold!"

So in came Nanna and Gustava and Gustava's Egg, and Goran shut the door.

"Present my subjects!" commanded the Queen of Clubs, and Goran saw that she was no longer a little card, but a lady as big as his grandmother. In front she still wore her blue and red and yellow dress, but in back she was all blue, every inch of her, with a pattern of gilt stars, and when she turned sideways she seemed to vanish, for she was only as thick as cardboard. But she was so proud and grand that Goran wished he had on his Sunday suit, with the long black trousers and the short black jacket with its big silver buttons, the waistcoat all covered with needlework flowers, and the raspberry pink neckerchief.

"This is Nanna, our Goat, your Majesty," he said.

"Goat, you may kiss my hand," said the Queen.

"I don't know whether I want to," replied rude Nanna, who had never been presented to a Queen before, and didn't know the proper way to behave.

"Mercy on us! What manners!" cried the Geraniums, blushing deep red that the Queen should be spoken to in that manner, in what they thought of as *their* house.

"But I wouldn't mind eating your yellow flower," continued Nanna. "I like to eat flowers." And she looked at the Geraniums, who nearly fainted.

"Your turn next," said the Queen to Gustava. She had heard gentlemen say that so often when they were playing *Skat* with her and her companions that she always repeated it when she could think of nothing else to say.

"Squawk! Cluck!" cried Gustava. "Would your Majesty like to see my beautiful child?" and she showed the Queen her Egg. "Just look, your Majesty! Have you ever seen anything more lovely? Such a pale brown color! Such an innocent expression! Perhaps your Majesty is also a mother?"

"Tick! Tock! Don't forget to wind me!" said the old Clock.

This is Nanna, our Goat, your Majesty.

"Gustava Hen talks too much," the fat Teapot in the corner cupboard told her daughters the Teacups. "When the Queen speaks to *you*, just say 'Yes, your Majesty,' and 'No, your Majesty,' and I dare say she will take you all to Court and find you handsome husbands among the Royal Coffeecups."

"Your Majesty should see my beautiful home," went on Gustava. "A nest of pure gold!" (She thought it was gold, but it was really yellow straw.)

"Just like my throne," replied the Queen. "Speaking of beautiful homes, you *should* see my Palace! There are fifty-three rooms!" (She said this because it was the highest number she knew, for there are fifty-three cards in the pack, counting the Joker who keeps all the cards amused when they are shut up in their box. And she had seen a room in the Palace, because she had been used in a game of *Skat* there, once in her early youth. But that was long, long ago.)

"My throne and the King's throne are pure gold, just like your nest, my good Gustava. And the walls are painted red and white, in swirls, like strawberries and cream. The stove has such a tall slender figure, and wears a golden crown. And then, just imagine, all the lamps are dripping with icicles at the same time that the floor is covered with blooming roses!" (For that is how she thought of the glass lusters on the lamps and the carpet on the floor.)

"Icicles! Ice! Freezing! *That* reminds me of our important message!" cried Nanna. "Your Snowman, Goran. He looks so dreadfully cold out there, we were afraid he would perish."

"Oh, yes! How could we have forgotten for so long! Cluck! Cluck! Cluck! He will certainly be frozen to death unless something is done quickly!"

"Do you mean to tell me that any one is out of doors on such a night as this?" questioned the Queen. "Have him brought in at once! Your turn next!" And she looked so severely at Goran that he felt his ears getting red.

So Goran and Nanna brought the Snowman in, while the Queen gave orders from the doorway, Gustava sat on her darling Egg to keep it warm, Mejau walked away with his tail as big as a bottle brush, and the Geraniums cried in chorus:

"Shut the door! Shut the door! We shall all catch cold!"

The Queen and the Snowman.

"Poor thing! How pale he is!" exclaimed the Queen. "And how dreadfully cold! Put him in a chair by the fire!"

The Snowman looked out of wondering sky-blue glass eyes, but said never a word, for he was very shy; and as he had only been born that afternoon, everything in the world was new to him.

"I want a drink!" cried the youngest Geranium; and: "Tick! Tock! Tick! Don't forget to wind me!" the old Clock repeated; but no one paid any attention to them.

"Your turn next!" said the Queen to Nanna. "Make a blaze, for this poor creature is nearly frozen." So with a clatter of tiny hoofs, Nanna built up the fire, only pausing to eat a twig or two, until even Mejau was nearly roasted.

But the poor Snowman was worse instead of better. His twig mouth still smiled bravely, and his blue eyes remained wide open, but tears seemed to pour down his cheeks, and he was growing thinner before their very eyes.

"If you please," he said in a timid voice, "I'm——"

"Give him a drink of something hot," advised the fat Teapot, and that reminded the youngest Geranium, who began screaming:

"I want a drink! I want a drink! I want a drink!"

"I'll be delighted to oblige with some nice warm milk," Nanna offered, so Goran milked a bowlful. But the Snowman could not drink it, and the tears ran faster and faster down his face.

"If you please——" he began again, faintly.

"We must put him to bed," the Queen interrupted, with a stern look at Gustava who was sitting on her darling Egg in the center of Grandmother's feather bed. "Your turn next!"

Grandmother's bed was built into the wall, like a cupboard. It was all carved with harebells and pinecones and kobolds and nixies. The kobolds are the elves who live in the mountain forests, and the nixies are water fairies who sit under the waterfalls playing upon their harps and making the sweetest music in the world. There was a big white feather bed on Grandmother's bed, and a big red feather bed on top of that, and two fat pillows stuffed with goose feathers. And above all this was a little shelf with two smaller feather beds and two smaller pillows, and that was Goran's bed. On dreadfully cold nights they pulled two little wooden doors shut, and there they were, quite warm and cozy—even quite stuffy, you and I might think! The doors of the bed were painted with pink tulips and red hearts, and Grandmother said it made her feel quite young and warm to look at them, and Goran said it made him feel quite young and warm too. And Gustava the Hen thought they were beautiful, so there she sat on her darling Egg, and as she could never think of more than one thing at a time, she had forgotten all about the Snowman, and was happily clucking this song to her Egg:

"Make a wreath, I beg,
For my darling Egg!

"Flowers blue as cloudless sky
When the summer Sun is high,
Harebells, little cups of blue,
Holding drops of crystal dew.

"Rain-wet pinks as sweet as spice,
Lilies white as snow and ice,
Lemon-colored lilies, too,
And the flax-flower's lovely blue.

"Strawberries sweet and red and small,
And the purple monkshood tall;
Let the moon-white daisies shine,
Bring the coral columbine.

"Weave the shining buttercup,
Bind the sweet wild roses up;
Poppies, red as coals of fire,
And the speckled foxglove spire.

"And the iris blue that gleams
Knee-deep in the foamy streams.
Bring the spruce cones brown and long."
(Thus ran on Gustava's song).

"Make a wreath, I beg,
For my darling Egg!"

"Make a wreath, I beg,
For Gustava's Egg,"

broke in Nanna the Goat impatiently:

"Why leave the Geraniums out?
Add the Teapot's broken spout,
Cheese, and brown potatoes, too;
Anything at all will do.

"Feathers from the feather bed,
Goran's mittens, warm and red,
And the flower the Queen holds up,
And the cracked blue china cup.

"But the Queen has said
Kindly leave that bed!"

So Gustava had to flop off the bed with a squawk, while Goran handed her her Egg, and then they put the poor Snowman, what was left of him, into Grandmother's bed, and pulled the eiderdown quilts over him.

"If you please," said the Snowman in a feeble whisper, "oh, if you *please*, I'm——"

"I know this is the right thing to do, because it is the way we always treat Snowmen at the Palace," broke in the Queen. To tell you the truth, she had never seen a Snowman in her life before, but she would never admit that she didn't know all about everything.

The Snowman looked at them with despairing sky-blue eyes, while his tears poured down, soaking Grandmother's pillow. He had tried desperately to tell them something, but they would none of them listen. Suddenly Goran knew what it was.

"I believe we're melting him," said Goran. "He needs air."

"I need air," said the Snowman, his face shining with hope.

"*Air?*" said the Queen. "Nonsense! He's had too much air. He needs a hot brick at his feet!"

"I need air," faltered the Snowman.

"*Air?* Nonsense!" cried the fat Teapot and all her Teacup daughters, hoping the Queen would hear, and take them back to the Palace with her.

"I need air," sighed the Snowman, and now he looked discouraged.

"Air? Brrr-rrr!" And Mejau squeezed himself under the chest of drawers, much annoyed with every one.

"I need air," breathed the Snowman, looking at Goran with imploring eyes.

"*Air?* Mercy on us, that will mean opening the door again!" And the Geraniums shivered in every leaf and petal.

But Goran had helped the poor Snowman, now nearly melted away, out of bed, and was leading him to the door.

"I need——" whispered the Snowman, and his voice was so faint that Goran could hardly hear it.

And there, because he was melting away so fast, his mouth fell out and lay on the floor, just a little bent twig.

Poor Snowman! Oh, poor Snowman! He could not make a sound now—he could only look at them, so sadly, so sadly!

But a little Mouse peeping with bright eyes out of its hole saw what had happened, and, since Mejau was nowhere in sight, ventured to squeak:

"Oh, please, Ma'am! Oh, please, Sir! The poor gentleman's mouth is lying on the floor!"

So the Queen picked it up and pressed it into place again, but by mistake she put it on wrong side up, so that instead of a pleasant smile the Snowman had the crossest mouth in the world, pulled far down at each corner.

And what a change it made in him!

Before, his voice had been a gentle whisper—now it was an angry bellow that made the Teacups shiver on their shelf and the Geraniums turn quite pale, and the little Mouse dive back with a squeak into her hole, thinking to herself: "Well, I *never*!"

"Here, you!" shouted the Snowman. "Get me out of here, and get me out quick. Hop along, my girl, and open the door! Your turn next!" (This was to the astonished Queen.) "Now, then, carry me out!"

"Tick! Tock! I'm feeling dreadfully run down," said the old Clock.

"Tick! Tock!

Wind the Clock!

Tock! Tick!

Wind it quick!

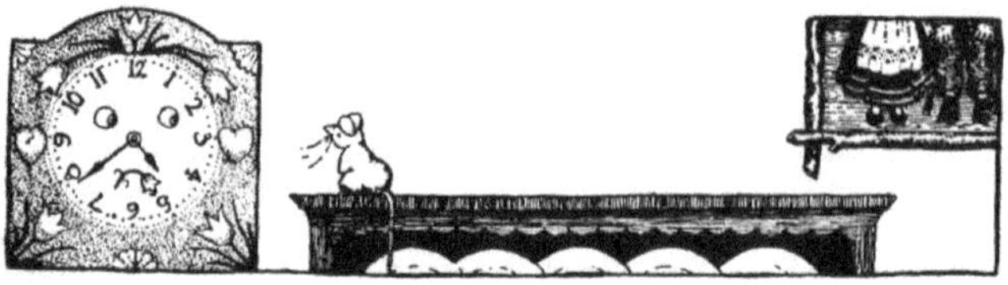

"Tick—Tock——" and he stopped talking.

The astonished Queen meekly threw open the door, and Goran carried the Snowman into the snowy darkness. Brr-rr! It was bitter cold!

"Now bring some snow and build me up," the Snowman ordered. "Leave the door open so that you can see—don't dawdle!"

The firelight from the open door shone on his blue glass eyes, and made two angry red sparks gleam in them. Goran and the Queen, Gustava and Nanna, scooped up handfuls and hoof-fuls and wing-fuls of newly fallen snow, and patted it on to the Snowman until he stuck out his chest more proudly than he had done in the first place, and he was so fat that he looked as if he were wearing six white fur coats, one on top of another. And all the time when he wasn't frightening the Queen half out of her wits by shouting: "Your turn next!" he kept muttering away to himself:

"Melt me over the fire! Smother me in a feather bed! Put a hot brick at my feet!"

It was when Goran was patting a little fresh snow on the Snowman's nose that he accidentally knocked his twig mouth off again. And this time it was put back right side up, so that the Snowman was as smiling as he had been in the beginning.

He stopped roaring. He stopped muttering. Did the fire die down? For the red sparks no longer gleamed in his gentle sky-blue eyes.

"Oh, thank you so much!" said the Snowman. "You have been so kind to me! And I know that you were trying to help me in the house. Forgive me for having been so cross! Will you please forgive me?"

And the Snowman looked so anxiously at Goran and the Queen and Nanna and Gustava that they all answered:

"Yes, yes, of course we will! And will you please forgive *us* for nearly melting you?"

"And now go in, for this lovely air is cold for you, I know."

"Oh, it is bitter cold!" agreed the Queen. "Brr-rrr! It is bitter cold."

Brr-rr! It was bitter cold!

Goran rubbed his eyes. Only a few red embers glowed in the fireplace. How stiff he was!

He must have slept in his chair all night, but he could not tell how late it was, for the Clock had stopped. He had forgotten to wind it, he remembered now.

There sat the Queen in her chair, but she was just a little card again.

Then he remembered the Snowman. He ran out of doors.

There the Snowman stood, as roly-poly as ever, with his twig mouth smiling and his sky-blue eyes wide open. He said nothing, but Goran felt they two understood each other.

What a night it had been! Could it all have been a dream? But now the night was over, and the storm was over; and, best of all, through the dim twilight he saw on the fjord far below him Neighbor Skylstad's rowboat, and seated in it, wrapped in her red shawl, his own dear grandmother coming home to him.

The Dream Coach stopped at the Princess's castle, then by road of stars to Goran's cottage in Norway next to the palace of the little Emperor, lastly to the house in France where Phillipe visited his Grandparents

A Bird Cage With tassels of Purple and Pearls

The Driver of the Dream Coach paused as he turned over the pages of the great white and gold book in which are kept the names of all those who have ridden or are to be given rides in the brightly painted Coach.

"I see," he said, addressing the little angels who helped him keep these records, "I see the name of the Little Chinese Emperor. And there is a cross opposite his name. Has he been naughty?" he asked. "Has he been picking the sacred lotus flowers of his honorable ancestors? Has he——"

"Oh, please," interrupted one of the smallest angels, "I put that cross there to remind me to tell you something about the Little Emperor. You see he hasn't been naughty—not exactly—but he's made a mistake. He doesn't understand," said the smallest angel, with his eyes round and serious.

"And can I help the Little Emperor understand?" asked the Driver of the Dream Coach.

"Of course you can!" cried the smallest angel, beaming brightly. "It's this way. The Little Chinese Emperor has a friend of mine fastened up in a cage, where he is very sad——"

"An angel in a cage?" asked the Driver. "I never heard of such a thing!"

"Well, not exactly an angel, a——"

But what it was, and how the Driver helped the little angel's friend——

That you shall hear.

The Little Emperor was dreadfully bored. He yawned so that his round little face, as round and yellow as a full moon, grew quite long, and his nose wrinkled up into soft yellow creases, like cream that is being pushed back by the skimmer from the top of a bowl of milk. His slanting black eyes shut up tight, and when they opened they were so full of tears that they sparkled like blackthorn berries wet with rain.

"Oh, dear! Oh, dear!" cried his aunt, Princess Autumn Cloud. "The Little Emperor is bored! What shall we do, oh, what shall we do to amuse him? For when he is bored, he very soon grows naughty, and when he is naughty—oh, *dear*!"

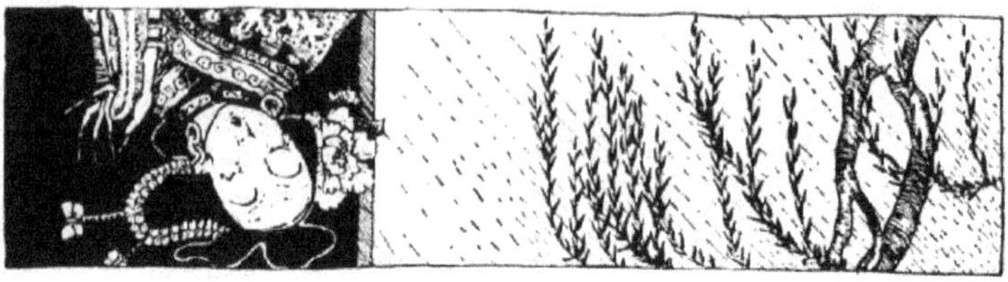

And she began to cry. But then she was always crying. When she was born her father and mother named her Bright Yellow Butterfly Floating In The Sunshine, but she cried so much that by the time she was five years old they saw that name wouldn't do at all, and changed it to Autumn Cloud Pouring Down Rain Upon The Sad Gray Sea.

She cried about anything. If her Lady-In-Waiting brought her a bowl of tea with honeysuckle blossoms in it, she would cry because they weren't jasmine flowers. If they were jasmine, she would cry because they weren't honeysuckle. When the peach trees bloomed she would cry because that meant that spring had come, and that meant summer would soon follow, and then autumn, and then the cold winter. "And oh, how cold the wind will be then, and how fast the snow will fall!" sobbed Princess Autumn Cloud, looking through her tears at the bright pink peach blossoms.

She cried because her sea-green jacket was embroidered with storks instead of bamboo trees.

She cried because they brought her shark-fin soup in a bowl of green lacquer with a gold dragon twisting around it, instead of a red lacquer bowl with a silver dragon.

She cried if the weather was hot.

She cried if the weather was cold.

And hardest of all she cried whenever the Little Emperor was naughty.

Whenever she began to cry a Lady-In-Waiting knelt in front of her and caught her tears in a golden bowl, for it never would have done to let them run down her cheeks, like an ordinary person's tears; they would have washed such deep roads through the thick white powder on her face. Every morning Princess Autumn Cloud (and, indeed, every lady in the Court of the Little Emperor) covered her face with honey in which white jasmine petals had been crushed to make it smell sweet, then when she was all sticky she put on powder until her face was as white as an egg. Then she painted on very surprised-looking black eyebrows and a little mouth as red and round as a blob of sealing wax. It looked just as if her mouth were an important letter that had to be sealed up to keep all sorts of secrets from escaping. Princess Autumn Cloud and Princess Gentle Breeze and Lady Gleaming Dragon Fly and Lady Moon Seen Through The Mist and all the rest of them would have thought it as shocking to appear without paint and powder covering up their faces as they would have thought it to appear without any clothes.

So Princess Autumn Cloud leaned over as if she were making a deep bow, and let her tears fall in a golden bowl, and then, because they were Royal tears, they were poured into beautiful porcelain bottles that were sealed up and placed, rows and rows and rows of them, in a room all hung with silk curtains embroidered with weeping willows.

"Oh, *what* shall be done to amuse the Little Emperor?" sobbed Princess Autumn Cloud. "Perhaps he would like some music!" And she clapped her hands, with their long, long fingernails covered with gold fingernail protectors.

So four fat musicians, dressed in vermilion silk and wearing big horn-rimmed spectacles to show how wise they were, came and kowtowed to the Little Emperor. That is, they got down on their knees, which was hard for them to do because they were so fat, and then, all together, knocked their heads on the floor nine times apiece to show their deep respect.

Then one beat on a drum, boom boom, and one clashed cymbals of brass together, crash *bang*, and one rang little bells of green and milk-white jade, and the oldest and fattest beat with mallets up and down the back of a musical instrument carved and painted to look like a life-sized tiger with glaring eyes and sharp white teeth.

The Little Emperor sprawled back in his big dragon throne under the softly waving peacock feather fans, stretched out his arms and legs, and yawned harder than ever.

Four fat Chinese musicians.

"Oh! Oh! Oh! *What* shall be done to amuse him?" wailed Princess Autumn Cloud, bursting into tears afresh. "Can *no* one suggest anything?"

And although the Mandarins and the Court Ladies thought to themselves that what they would really like to suggest for such a spoiled little boy would be to send him to bed without his supper, they none of them dared say so, but tried to look very solemn and sympathetic.

"Would the Little Old Ancestor enjoy some sweetmeats?" suggested Lady Lotus Blossom. "Old Ancestor" is what you call the Emperor if you are properly brought up, *and* polite, *and* Chinese.

So Gentlemen-In-Waiting came and kowtowed and offered the Little Emperor lacquered boxes of crystallized ginger, of sugared sunflower seeds, and of litchi nuts. But do you think he was interested? Not at all. He would not even look at them.

"The wind is blowing hard. Would it amuse the Little Old Ancestor to watch the kites fly?" asked old Lord Mighty Swishing Dragon's Tail.

The Little Emperor didn't know whether it would or not. However, he couldn't be more bored than he was already, so he climbed down from his throne and went out into the windy autumn garden.

First marched the musicians, beating on drums to let every one know that the Emperor was coming.

Then came the Court Ladies tottering along on their "golden lilies," which is what they call their tiny feet that have been bound up tightly to keep them small ever since the ladies were babies.

Then the Mandarins with their long pigtails and their padded silk coats whose big sleeves held fans and tobacco and bags of betel nuts and sheets of pale green and vermilion writing paper.

Then Princess Autumn Cloud in a jade green gown embroidered with a hundred lilac butterflies, a lilac jacket, and pale rose-colored trousers tied with lilac ribbons. In her ears, around her arms, and on her fingers were jade and pearls, and her rose-colored shoes were trimmed with tassels of pearls and were so tiny that she could hardly hobble. In her shiny black hair she wore on one side a big peony, the petals made of mother-of-pearl and the leaves of jade. Each petal and leaf was on a fine wire so that when she moved her head they trembled as real flowers do when the wind blows over them. On the other side were two jade butterflies that trembled too. In front of her, walking backward, went her Lady-In-Waiting holding the golden tear bowl, in case the Princess should suddenly begin to cry.

And last of all, surrounded by his Gentlemen-In-Waiting, came the Little Emperor, dressed from head to foot in yellow, the Imperial color, so that he looked like a yellow baby duckling. And as he came every one in the Palace and in the Garden had to stop whatever they were doing—gossiping, teasing the Royal monkeys, chewing betel nuts, or sweeping up dead leaves—and kneel down and knock their heads on the ground until he had passed.

How the wind was blowing! It sent the willow branches streaming, it wrinkled the lake water and turned the lotus leaves wrong side out, it scattered the petals of the chrysanthemums. It tossed the kites high in the air. How brightly their colors shone against the gray sky! Some were made to look like pink and yellow melons with trailing leaves, some were like warriors in vermilion, some were golden fish, others were black bats, and the biggest one of all was a great blue-green dragon.

As for the Little Emperor, he took one look at them and then yawned so hard that they were afraid he would dislocate his jaw.

A little brown bird the color of a dead leaf had been hopping about on the ground under the chrysanthemums looking for something for its supper, and now suddenly flew up into a willow tree and began to sing.

The Little Emperor clapped his hands, and all his servants dropped on their knees and began to kowtow.

"Catch me that little brown bird with the beautiful song!" he said. He stopped yawning, and his eyes grew bright with eagerness.

"But, Little Old Ancestor, that is such a plain little bird," said his aunt timidly. "Surely you would rather have a cockatoo as pink as a cloud at dawn, or a pair of lovebirds as green as leaves in spring——"

The rude Little Emperor paid not the slightest attention to her, but stamped his foot and shouted:

"*Catch me that little brown bird!*"

So his servants chased the poor little fluttering bird with butterfly nets. The wind whipped their bright silk skirts, and their pigtails streamed out behind, and they puffed and panted, for they were most of them very fat.

His servants chased the bird with butterfly nets.

And at last the bird was caught, and put in a cage trimmed with tassels of purple silk and pearls, with drinking cup and seed cup made like the halves of plums from purple amethysts on brown amber twigs with green jade leaves.

For a time the Little Emperor was delighted with his new pet, and every day he carried it in its cage when he went for a walk. But it never sang, only beat against the bars of its cage, or huddled on its perch, so presently he grew tired of it, and it was hung up in its cage in a dark corner of one of the Palace rooms, where he soon forgot all about it.

How could the little bird sing? It was sick for the wide blue roads of the air, for wet green rice fields where the coolies stand with bare legs, sky-blue shirts, and bamboo hats as big as umbrellas, for the yellow rivers, and the mountains bright with red lilies. How could it sing in a cage? But sometimes it tried to cry to them: "Let me out! Please, *please* let me out! I have never done anything to harm you! I am so unhappy I think my heart is breaking! *Please* let me go free!"

"What a sweet song!" everybody would say. "Run and tell the Little Emperor that his bird is singing again."

After a while the little bird realized that they did not understand, and it tried no longer, but drooped, dull-eyed and silent, in its cage.

One night the Little Emperor had a dream. Perhaps you won't wonder when I tell you what he had for supper.

First he had tea in a bowl of jade as round and white as the moon, heaped up with honeysuckle flowers.

Then, in yellow lacquer boxes, sugared seeds, sunflower and lotus flower and watermelon seeds, boiled walnuts, and lotus buds.

Then velvety golden peaches and purple plums with a bloom of silver on them.

Pork cooked in eleven different ways: chopped, cold, with red beans and with white beans, with bamboo shoots, with onions, and with cherries, with eggs, with mushrooms, with cabbage, and with turnips.

Ducks and chickens stuffed with pine needles and roasted.

Smoked fish.

Shrimps and crabs, fried together.

Shark fins.

Boiled birds' nests.

Porridge of tiny yellow seeds like bird seed.

Cakes in the shapes of seashells, fish, dragons, butterflies, and flowers.

Chrysanthemum soup, steaming in a yellow bowl with a green dragon twisting around it.

Not one other thing did that poor Little Emperor have for his supper!

When he was so full that he couldn't hold anything more, not even one sugared watermelon seed, they took off his silk napkin embroidered with little brown monkeys eating pink and orange persimmons. He was so sleepy that he did not even stamp his feet when they washed his face and hands. Then they took off his red silk gown embroidered with gold dragons and blue clouds and lined with soft gray fur, his yellow silk shirt and his red satin shoes with their thick white soles. But he went to bed in his pale yellow pantaloons, tied around the ankles with rose-colored ribbons.

I must tell you about his bed. It was made of brick, and inside of it a small fire was built to keep the Little Emperor warm. On top of this three yellow silk mattresses were placed, then silk sheets, red, yellow, green, blue, and violet, then a coverlet of yellow satin embroidered with stars. Under his head were pillows stuffed with tea leaves; and above him was a canopy of yellow silk, embroidered with a great round moon whose golden rays streamed down the yellow silk curtains drawn around him.

He fell asleep, and this is what he dreamed.

The long golden rays seemed to turn into the bars of a cage. Yes, he was in a huge cage! He tried frantically to get out! He beat against the bars! Then he saw what looked like the roots of trees, and brown tree trunks, a grove all around the cage. But the trees moved and stepped about, and, looking up the trunks, instead of leaves he saw feathers, and still farther, sharp beaks, and then bright eyes looking at him. They were birds!

What he had thought were the roots of trees were their claws, and the trunks of the trees were their legs. But what enormous birds! They were as big as men, while he was as small as a bird.

"Let me out!" he shouted. "Don't you know I am the Emperor, and every one must obey me? Let me out, I say!"

"Ah, he is beginning to sing," said one bird to another.

"Not a very musical song. Too shrill by far! Take my advice, wring his neck and roast him. He would make a tender, juicy morsel for our supper."

"Please, *please* let me out!"

"Oh, let me out! Please, *please* let me out!" cried the poor Little Emperor in terror.

"He is singing more sweetly now," remarked one of the birds.

"Too loud! Quite ear-splitting!" said a lady bird, fluffing out her breast feathers and lifting her wings to show how sensitive she was.

"If he were mine I should pluck him. His little yellow silk trousers would line my nest so softly."

"Oh, please, *please* set me free!"

"Really, his song is growing quite charming! But one can't stand listening to it all day."

And with a great whir and flap and rustle of wings the birds flew away and left him in his cage, alone.

He called for help and threw himself against the bars until he was exhausted. Then bruised, panting, his heart nearly breaking out of his body, he lay on the floor of the cage. Finally, growing hungry and thirsty, he looked in his seed and water cups, drank a little lukewarm water, and ate a dry bread crumb. Now and then birds came and looked at him. Some of them tried to catch his pigtail with their beaks or claws.

Next day the Little Emperor was thoughtful. Could it be, he wondered, that a little bird's nest was as dear to it as his own bed with its rainbow coverlets and its moon and stars was to him? That a little bird liked ripe berries and cold brook water as much as he liked ripe peaches and tea with jasmine flowers? That a little bird was as frightened when he tried to catch its tail in his fingers as he was when the birds tried to catch his pigtail?

And then he thought of how he had felt when the lady bird had wanted his pantaloons to line her nest, and, hot with shame, he remembered his glistening jewel-bright blue cloak made of thousands of kingfishers' feathers. It had made him miserable to think of their taking his clothes, but suppose his clothes grew on him as their feathers did on them? How would he have felt then, hearing the bird say: "*I* should pluck him. His little silk trousers would line my nest so softly"?

He went to bed thinking about his little brown bird, and before he shut his eyes he made up his mind to set it free in the morning.

Then he fell asleep, and once again he dreamed that he was in the golden cage.

Whir-rr! One of the great birds flew down by the cage door. With his claw he unfastened it—opened it!

Oh, how exciting! The Little Emperor tore out, so afraid he would be stopped and put back in the cage!

Oh, how he ran across the room and through the open door! Free! He was free! Tears rushed to his eyes, and his heart felt as if it would burst with happiness.

But it was winter. The garden was deep in snow that was falling as if it would never stop. The peaches and plums were gone, and the lotus pond was frozen hard as stone.

The Little Emperor had never been out in the snow before except when he was dressed in his warm padded clothes, with one Gentleman-In-Waiting carrying his porcelain stove, and another bringing tea, and a third with cakes in a box of yellow lacquer, and a fourth holding between the snowflakes and the Imperial head a great, moss-green umbrella. So small and helpless in so big and cold a world, what could a little boy find to eat or drink? Where could he warm himself? He ran frantically through the snow. The rose-colored ribbons that tied his pantaloons came untied and trailed behind him, and the cold snow went up his bare legs.

Pausing to catch his sobbing breath, he looked up to see the thick snow sliding from a pine tree branch, and jumped aside just in time to keep from being buried beneath it. Then on he plunged again, growing with each step more weak and cold and hungry; stopping now and then to call for help in a quavering voice that grew feebler every time; blinking back the tears that froze on his lashes as he tried to remember that emperors must never cry; then struggling on through the blinding snow, a little boy lost and alone.

Then, as it began to grow dark, he saw two great lanterns shining through the snow, coming slowly nearer. Perhaps his aunt and his Chief Gentleman-In-Waiting, Lord Mighty Swishing Dragon's Tail (Lord Dragon Tail, for short) had missed him and had come with lanterns to look for him! He tried to go toward them, to call, but he was too exhausted to move or make a sound.

And then, imagine his terror when he realized that the glowing green lights were not lanterns at all, but the eyes of a great crouching animal—a cat!

Gathering all his strength for one last desperate effort, he tried to run. But with a leap the cat was after him, and with a paw now rolled into a velvet ball, now unsheathing sharp curved claws, tapped him first on one side, then on the other, nearly let him go, caught him again with one bound, and with a harder blow sent him spinning into stars and darkness.

Some one was shaking him. Was it the cat? The Little Emperor opened his eyes and saw the frightened face of Princess Autumn Cloud bending over him, as yellow as a lemon, for she had jumped up out of bed when she heard him cry out in his sleep, and there hadn't been time to put on the honey and the powder, to paint on the surprised black eyebrows or the round red mouth.

"Wake up, wake up, Little Old Ancestor!" she was crying as she shook him. "You're having a bad dream!"

"Aren't you the cat?" asked the Little Emperor, who wasn't really awake yet.

"Certainly *not*, Little Old Ancestor!" replied his aunt, rather offended.

The Little Emperor climbed out of his bed. The room was full of the still white light that comes from snow, and looking out of the window he saw that the plum trees and the cherry trees looked as if they had blossomed in the night, the snow lay so white and light on every twig. Softly the snow fell, deep, deep it lay, and the people who passed by his windows went as silently as though they were shod in white velvet.

The Little Emperor thought of his dream, and decided that his little bird might suffer and die if he let it go free before winter was over. But he explained to the bird, and tried to make it happier.

"When summer comes, you shall fly away into the sky," he told it. He brought it fruit and green leaves to peck at, talking to it gently. And the little bird seemed to understand. The dull eyes grew brighter; and though it never sang it sometimes chirped as if it were trying to say: "Thank you."

On the first night of summer when the moon lay like a great round pearl in the deep blue sea of the sky, the Little Emperor slept, and dreamed again that the cage door opened for him and let him go free. But oh, what happiness now, happiness almost too great for a little boy to bear.

Peonies were in bloom, each petal like a big seashell, and blue butterflies floated over them in the warm sunshine. Half hidden in the grass the Little Emperor found a great purple fruit—a mulberry. How good it was!

The dewy spider webs glistened like the great tinsel Bridge to Heaven they built for him on every birthday. How happy he was! How happy! Free and safe! With the sun to warm him and the breeze to cool him; with food tumbling down from Heaven or the mulberry trees, he wasn't sure which, with a crystal clear dewdrop to drink on every blade of grass. How happy he was!

The lake was full of great rustling leaves and big pink lotus flowers. Venturing out on one of the leaves, he paddled his feet over its edge in the gently lapping water. Then, climbing into one of the pink blossoms, he lay, so happy, so happy, looking up at the blue-green dragon flies darting overhead, and rocking gently in his rosy boat.

No, it was not the lotus flower that rocked him on the water. It was Princess Autumn Cloud who was gently shaking him, and saying: "Wake up, if you please, dear Little Old Ancestor!" And hard as it is to believe, she was really smiling. The Little Emperor had been so good lately, and then it was such a beautiful day!

He could not wait until after breakfast to let his little brown bird go free. As soon as he was dressed he ran as fast as he could to the room where the bird cage hung. Pat-a-pat-pat went his little feet in their blue satin shoes, and thud, thud! puff, puff! his fat old Gentlemen-In-Waiting lumbered along behind him.

"I've come to set you free!" he whispered, as he carried the cage with its tassels of purple and pearls out into the beautiful day. For one minute he wanted to cry, for he had grown to love the little bird. But he remembered again that emperors must not cry. He opened the door of the cage.

"Little Old Ancestor's bird has flown away!" cried the Mandarins.

"It has flown so high in the sky that we can hardly see it," the Court Ladies answered; and they all wished that the Little Emperor would stop gazing up into the sky at the little dark speck, so that they might go in and have their breakfasts.

But the Little Emperor, the empty bird cage in his hand, still looked up. High, high in the sky! And now, really, he could no longer see it. But a thread of song dropped down to him, a silver thread of song, a golden thread of love between the hearts of a little bird and a little boy.

"Thank you, oh, thank you, my Little Emperor!"

"King" Philippe's Dream

Up into the sky rose the hundred horses and their great Coach, until the roof of the Little Emperor's Palace with its bright yellow tiles looked only as big as a yellow autumn leaf—as a jasmine petal—as nothing at all! And along the Road of Stars they galloped, while notes of music sprayed from the wheels of the Coach, and, dropping to earth, gave the nightingales ideas for beautiful new songs.

On through the sky and above the earth until the night was over, and at last, instead of a road, the hundred horses were galloping along a river. All along the river bank tall poplars rustled and whispered in the wind of the Coach's passing, and little waves, stirred up by the horses' hoofs, slapped against the small houses that rose from the water, small pink houses and blue houses and white red-roofed houses, each with its rowboat tied to its steps. White swans and green ducks rocked on the ripples, their feathers gilded by sunshine, for it was bright day now, and the rain that had been pouring down had stopped. It was bright day, and yet no one saw the Dream Coach except a little French boy, whose eyes were falling shut in one little pink cottage.

"Philippe! Philippe!" the Driver called. "One last dream is left for you!"

What was Philippe's dream?

That you shall hear.

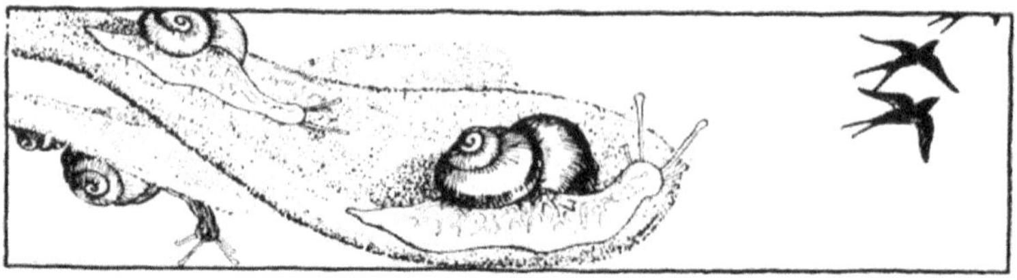

"Hold still then, my little monkey!"

"But mother," wailed Philippe, "I have the soap in my eye!"

"Soap is it, my angel?" asked his mother, lifting his face in her two wet hands. "Oh, but there is really no soap at all to speak about, just a bubble or two of suds. *There!*" and with the corner of her apron she wiped away the thick white lather around his eyelashes, so that Philippe looked like a little boy made of snow, except for his eyes which were large and brown and filled with tears from the painful smarting. From head to ankles he was covered with a froth of soapsuds, and his feet had stirred the warm water in the bottom of the wooden tub into rainbow-tinted mounds of bubbles which grew and grew and cascaded over the sides with a tiny fizzing sound.

"You are giving our young one a very thorough tubbing," remarked Philippe's father. He was sitting under the narrow window of their cottage, cutting the yellow-white sprouts from a bag of potatoes which he intended to plant in the dark of the next moon.

"Indeed I am. I shall scrub and rub and polish until he looks like a wax image, or as pink and shining as the inside of the seashell his Uncle Pablôt sent him from Paimpol."

Philippe's father held a large brown potato at arm's length, and, regarding it with his head cocked to one side, said: "Very fine! Yes, very fine!"

"A good size," agreed his wife, looking over her shoulder, while she absently bored into the ear of her long-suffering son with a bit of soapy rag.

"Yes—but I was thinking rather of Philippe's Uncle Pablôt. It is he who is very fine, a grand gentleman who carries a gold-headed cane and has traveled far—to the very borders of our beloved France, and even beyond, so I hear."

"Oh, very much beyond! He has been in every country in the world, according to the wonderful stories he tells, and the world, Pierre, I understand to be of a tremendous bigness; indeed, if what I am told is the truth, it must be three or four times as big as our own country!"

"Is that so?" replied Pierre doubtfully, starting to cut the pallid sprouts again with quick motions of his work-hardened hands. "It may all be the truth, my good wife, but I have always taken the words of Pablôt with a grain of salt; I think, for that matter, that he is a little inclined to blow."

"'Blow'?" asked Philippe from his tub. "I thought it was only the wind that could blow."

But of course no one answered him, for he was only a little boy, and not expected to understand; instead, his father bent over his bag of potatoes to hide his smile, and his mother remembered that the *pot-au-feu* (which is a thick soup made of odds and ends and bits and scraps and almost everything you can think of mixed with water in a large pot and left on the fire to bubble sluggishly for many hours) needed stirring right away.

"Take care," warned her husband, "that you do not drop soap into the soup from your wet hands, for I know of nothing that gives it a more curious flavor."

"Just the same," said Philippe's mother, turning from the hearth, her cheeks flushed rosy red by the bright, hot embers, "just the same, it is a good thing that our little one should be invited to meet such a fine gentleman. It will teach him how to say the most ordinary thing elegantly, and how to carry his head high as if he were a born dandy. Philippe, repeat to your father the little speech you are to say when you meet your uncle."

"Good health to you, my dear and illustrated uncle! It gives——"

"No, no, my pet, 'my dear and *illustrious* uncle,' and was there not something that you forgot?"

"Yes, Mother. I forgot to make my bow. Shall I make a new beginning?"

"Do so."

Whereupon Philippe bent nearly double over the edge of the tub, scattering drops of water upon the floor.

"Good health to you, my dear and illustrious uncle. It gives me the most great pleasure to have—*eugh!* soap in my mouth.... *Ptu!*——"

"Wait, then, until you are dressed in the new suit I have sewn for you," and his mother, taking an earthen jar of water from the side of the fire where it had been put to warm, poured it over his head, leaving him no longer a snow boy, but a boy made of the shiniest china you can imagine. "Is that pleasant, my brave one?"

"It is warm, like rain," said Philippe, lifting his arms above his head. "I will not need another washing for a long, long time, will I, Mother?"

Philippe's grandparents lived the distance of twelve fields, a small woods, three stiles, and the width of a brook from his own home. Just how far that is, is hard to say. You see it makes such a difference whom you ask. Ask the swallows and they will tell you airily that it is no distance at all, just a flick of the wing, and you are there. But ask the snails who live under the broad leaves of the flowering mulleins, and after pondering a long time, they will tell you that it gives them a headache to think of such a tremendous distance, that it would surely take several lifetimes to travel so far, and as for themselves, they would consider it very foolish to start out on such a dangerous adventure when there were plenty of young lettuces so close at hand! To a small boy of eight, it was quite a long journey, taken alone, particularly when he could not take the short cut by wriggling through the tangled copse for fear of tearing his new suit, or being covered with last year's burrs and barbed seeds of the undergrowth. But he reached his Grandparents' house at last.

It was a little house built by the side of a river, actually touching the water on one side, so that you could step out of a door, down a step, and into a rowboat. And there were white swans and yellow-breasted ducks with bronze-green backs swimming in the reflection of the pink walls. On the land side was a poplar tree, very tall and dressed in silvery blue leaves, standing erect like a giant soldier on guard before a toy house. Once Philippe's Grandfather had explained to him how he could tell the time of day by the shadow this tree cast: when it struck across the chimney at the corner of the house, it was time to go into the fields; when it crossed the front door, it was time to enter therein for the midday meal, and when it pointed out toward the fields, that was a signal for Grandmother to ring the great bell that would call the workers home.

"And what," Philippe had asked, "do you do, Grandfather, when the sun is under the clouds, and there is no shadow to tell the time?"

"Well, then we must needs look at the clock which ticks on the mantelshelf over the fire," Grandfather said with a twinkle of his old, blue eyes, eyes half hidden by the tufts of white eyebrows.

Although the day had commenced unusually fine, and the calm, blue sea of sky had been without an island reef or bar of cloud to wreck the golden galleon of the sun, by the time Philippe had been tubbed, scrubbed, dressed in his best, had been rehearsed in his address to his uncle, kissed good-by, and given a little nosegay of pansies and lilies of the valley in a paper twist for his Grandmother, and had crossed the twelve fields and picked his way carefully through the woods to avoid the sharp brambles that reached out after him with long and sinuous arms—by the time all this had come to pass, and Philippe was actually in sight of his grandparents' cottage, it began to rain from a sky as heavily gray as it had been brightly blue before. It started so suddenly that Philippe had to run across the last field to keep the big drops from ruining his new black velvet cap.

The inside of the house was very dark, with only two windows, like half-closed eyes, looking out on the world. Through these windows entered shafts of pale, watery light that cut blue paths in the wreaths of wood smoke creeping around the rafters. Pots, pans, and kettles of burnished copper hung from hooks in the ceiling, and mirrored in tiny points the flames leaping on the hearth. It was like another world, small but complete, inside Grandmother's and Grandfather's house: the floor was the earth itself, trampled until it was as hard as brick, the wreaths of smoke were thin clouds flung across a dark sky where yellow and red stars winked and twinkled. At one end of the room, where Grandmother and Anjou, the cat, were busy preparing dinner over the bright fire, it was gay and warm: *Day*;

but at the farther end, where Grandfather sat stroking his long white beard, it was dark and chilly: *Night.*

When Philippe entered, he had to blink his eyes for some time before he could adjust himself to the darkness. Then he handed his Grandmother the bouquet he had carried so carefully, politely wishing her health and happiness.

There were tears in Grandmother's eyes as she bent over and kissed her Grandson's pink and shining cheek, but then there were always tears in Grandmother's eyes—why, Philippe never could understand. Did she weep because of the stinging smoke that the chimney seemed too small to carry off? Or because she was sad? Not sad, thought Philippe, or Grandmother would not be all the time smiling.

"Hey-O!" sang Grandmother in her high little voice, dropping a tear in the yellow heart of a purple pansy. "What pretty flowers you have brought me, my Philippe, and see, here is a raindrop in one of them shining as prettily as a glass bead!"

Philippe did not like to tell her that it was her own tear.

"Then it is raining out?" she asked. "It will make a wet home-coming for your uncle, but it is lovely, nevertheless, and if it comes down hard enough, it will make the river flow along more happily than it has for a long day. Won't that be beautiful, Philippe?"

"Yes, Grandmother Marianne," Philippe agreed politely, and then asked: "When will my Uncle Pablôt be here? Mother has taught me what to say when I make my bow to him, and if he is too long in coming, I am afraid that I may forget it."

"He will come," said Grandmother, "when he has a mind to."

"And is he coming from a great distance, maybe all the way from Paris?" (Philippe thought that Paris was the only city in the world, built on the world's very edge.)

"Maybe, and then maybe not," Grandmother told him. "There is no telling where your uncle will come from; he is apt to blow in from any quarter."

"Ah, then that explains it!" remarked Philippe innocently. "Father said he always thought Uncle Pablôt was a little inclined to blow."

"Now did he!" Grandmother was frowning and smiling at one and the same time. "Have you spoken to your Grandfather yet?"

"I did not know that Grandfather Joseph was home; I did not see him," said Philippe truthfully.

"Use your young eyes sharply and look into every corner," advised Grandmother. "Anjou!" she cried warningly, "you will burn your nose if you get too close to that roasting duck."

Philippe gazed into the farthest corner of the room where he saw two dim spots of white glowing like snow in the night; he had to advance quite near before he could be sure that what he saw was the long white hair and the long white beard of Grandfather.

"Good day, Grandfather Joseph," said Philippe, bowing low before the old man who sat huddled in a chair, the arms of which were worn shiny by the grip of thin fingers.

"'Good day'? A very *bad* day, Grandson. Though I no longer hear nor see as I used to, I can feel that it is raining. Tell me, is it raining?"

"Yes, Grandfather," replied Philippe from the top of a churn where he had climbed to look out of the small window at the river. "It is falling so hard that the raindrops are bouncing from the surface of the water." Remembering what his Grandmother had told him, he added, "It will make the river flow along more happily than it has for a long time, and that will be very beautiful!"

"*Horrible!*" said Grandfather with a sigh that was almost too soft to be heard. "It makes me feel weak clear through," he continued. "Give me the sharp cold and the sparkling frost when the river freezes so hard that it cracks and roars like a cannon. When I was a boy, I used to spread my cape and let the wind push me across the slippery ice—— This soft weather will be the end of me!"

There were three people living in the house that Philippe visited; besides Grandmother and Grandfather, there was little Avril, their grandniece, and therefore Philippe's cousin. Avril was a child of tender beauty, younger than Philippe, quite a baby in the sight of eyes that were eight long years old. Avril was very shy, so shy that she had hidden under the table when Philippe had entered the door, and it was not until he had paid his respects to Grandmother and Grandfather that he saw her there, peeking out at him like a flower from the dark shadow of a garden wall. "Hello, my little cousin," said Philippe with a grand and grown-up air. "Would you like to play a very important game with me that I have just thought of?"

Avril laughed her pleasure.

It was a most excellent game, so Philippe thought. He was King, enthroned on the churn, and Avril was his slave, and had to bring him anything he might request, with the penalty of having her head chopped off if she failed. King Philippe had just commanded the brightest star in the heavens to be brought him, when there was all at once a loud rapping and rattling of the wooden latch. The door flew open before anyone had time to answer, and a gust of chilly wind swept through the room, breaking the weaving rings of smoke, making the fire leap up the chimney, causing Grandmother in her excitement to drop the wooden spoon into the pudding, and even waving Grandfather's beard like a white flag.

"*Behold!* I am here!" cried Uncle Pablôt from the threshold, withdrawing his right arm from the voluminous folds of his cape and making a magnificent sweeping gesture ending with his fingertips being pressed lightly against his expanded chest.

"So I see," said Grandfather in a thin, complaining voice from his dark corner. "Close the door," he pleaded, tucking the end of his waving beard into his blue smock. "Close the door—the rain makes me feel very weak——"

But no one paid the least bit of attention to him. Grandmother ran forward with squeaking noises of delight, throwing her arms around the newcomer, draping him with a link of sausage, which she had forgotten to put down in her hurry, in the manner of a necklace. Avril shyly retreated beneath the table again, and Philippe tried desperately to remember the pretty sentences with which he was to address the great man. He was in the very middle of trying to remember when his Grandmother took him by the hand.

"And here is your little nephew," said Grandmother, "who has come all by himself a great distance to welcome you."

Philippe stared dumbly, wishing that he had had the presence of mind to slip under the table with Avril.

"*Come!* What do you say to your uncle, Philippe?" asked Grandmother.

"I forget what I say," answered Philippe miserably, "but I am very glad to see you, my—my——Ah! Now it comes to me!" And he started again: "Good health to you, my dear and illustrious uncle. It gives me the most——"

"Fiddlesticks!" interposed Uncle Pablôt, laughing.

"—the most great pleasure to welcome you, and——"

"Yes, yes—" said Uncle Pablôt, cutting him short again. "But what do you say to this?" and he reached into the folds of his cape and handed Philippe something small and shining.

"What is it?" asked Philippe.

"Ho! That is better. At least you did not learn that by heart, did you, my boy? Here, I will show you." Whereupon he put the bright present to his lips and blew a shrill blast that rattled the pots and made Grandmother drop her sausages in alarm. (She dusted them very carefully before putting them in the hot pan that was waiting to cook them.)

"A *whistle*!" shouted Philippe, dancing with joy. Then he ducked under the table to show his beautiful new present to Avril.

"And here is a present for the other little one," said Uncle Pablôt, handing the shyly smiling girl a toy spade with a bright green handle and a wreath of early spring flowers painted on the tiny blade.

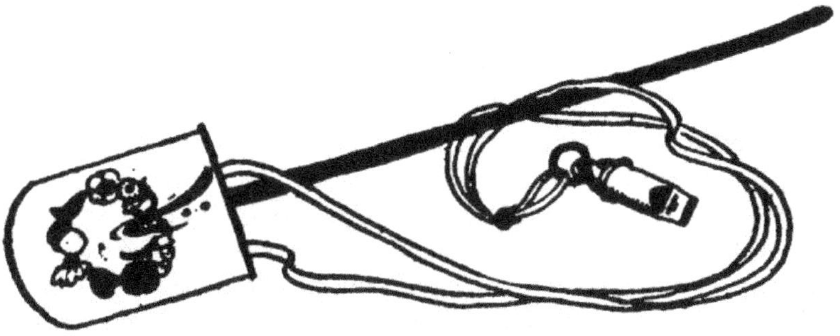

What a feast they had in honor of their distinguished guest!

"I suppose," said Grandmother to Uncle Pablôt, "that you have traveled a great distance since last you visited us?"

"Yes, yes," said Uncle Pablôt, flourishing the wing of a duck. "I have breezed about a bit, here, there, and everywhere. Would you like to hear a little about my travels?"

"Oh, *please*!" begged Philippe, although the question had not been addressed to him.

"Now there is India," commenced Uncle Pablôt, "a very hot country, but as gay as a circus——" And over the roast duck he told them many things in his soft and flowing voice, of elephants, their enormous bodies painted brilliantly in curlicues, circles, and zigzags, swaying through narrow streets like clumsy ships of the land, ridden by dark-skinned potentates robed in ivory satin and scarlet brocades, wearing precious jewels more sparkling than broken bits of colored glass ... of softly stepping and treacherous tigers prowling in deep jungles, of lions and leopards, crouching panthers and laughing hyenas and all manner of beasts ... of birds with emerald crests, sapphire wings, breasts of flaming orange, long, sweeping tails and screaming falsetto voices that seemed to shatter the air into sharp and hurtling splinters ... of gorilla fathers with so terrible a power in their long arms that they could uproot a tree as easily as one would pick a dandelion, and gorilla mothers holding babies to their breasts as gently and lovingly as any human mothers ... of chattering pink monkeys shouting in derisive laughter from their hiding places in the tree tops at passers-by. Leaving the wildness of the tropic forests, he told them of queer-shaped temples and pagodas, lifting to the blue of the sky, made of stone carved as beautifully as lace, where lived the leering and laughing gods of the heathen.

By the time Grandmother had put the crisp green lettuces on the table, Uncle Pablôt had carried his little audience to far-away China and, without so much as a "by your leave," into the gardens of mandarins and emperors where jasmine filled the air with sweetness, and rose and white peonies bowed their heavy heads around the lily ponds. Far away and far away they flew on Uncle Pablôt's winged words: over snowy mountains tinted with the pink and lavender radiance of the dawn, through the fiery furnace of desert sands where haughty camels plodded their weary course to the beat of Arab drum and the mystical rhythm of Arab song, up broad rivers where crocodiles basked in the sun ... past cities with towers and turrets, through the courtyards of palace and castle, into the riot of crowded markets with their laughter and shouting, buying and selling, into a land where the streets were water, where the buildings had wings that turned and turned, where the men and boys wore tight little jackets of velvet fastened with brass buttons, and trousers as big as two sacks sewn together. "Oh, yes," said Uncle Pablôt, "and they all wear wooden shoes so that they can walk safely across the streets of water without sinking."

"Remarkable!" said Grandmother.

"If true," said Grandfather, but he spoke so low that every one thought that he was merely choking, and paid no attention to him.

"More!" pleaded Philippe.

"And I was in England the other day," continued Uncle Pablôt, who needed little urging, "where I visited the Royal Family. That is nothing," he said, in answer to a look of proud astonishment from Grandmother. "I have a great many acquaintances in all walks of life. Once I mussed up the hair of a prince and ran off with the parasol of a duchess, just by way of a little joke, you know. Did I ever tell you——"

But if he ever had, he told them again, and at such length that, though the dinner had come to an end, and Grandmother had cleared away the dishes and given Anjou a saucer of milk and a bone, he was still telling them this and other monstrous adventures in his quick, easy voice. How thrilling it all was to Philippe. It seemed to him that the gay words flew from his uncle's mouth and over his head like flocks of wild birds. Some of them were quite ordinary little words, as sparrows are ordinary little birds, but others were long and strange like the queer birds his uncle had told him about. Or again—this tale of other lands and peoples was like music to which the crackling of the fire and the drip, drip of the rain outside made a soothing accompaniment. He tried hard to keep his eyes and ears wide open, but, to tell the truth, he had eaten very heartily of Grandmother's delicious dinner, and that, with the darkness of the room, the lullaby singsong of his uncle's voice, and the soft purring of Anjou, made him heavy-headed and in danger of falling into sleep at any moment. Voices came to him through the fog of smoke, sounding far, far away. He heard his uncle say, "But you, Grandfather Joseph, you should go about the world a bit and see for yourself these wonderful things."

"I am content," replied a soft, old voice.

"Yes, you are content to stay where you are put, or at best to drift around a bit, eh?"

And then the old man saying, "I drift—I drift—I drift——"

Maybe it was then that Philippe went to sleep, or, on the other hand, maybe it was then that Philippe overcame his drowsiness and woke up to a new interest in things. Certainly, strange and exciting happenings took place in rapid succession.

It started with Grandmother going to the window where she stood on tiptoe and looked out at the river. "Oh," she cried, and her voice was younger and happier than Philippe had ever heard it before. "Oh! The river has grown up; never before have I seen my darling child so strong and beautiful. And how he runs and laughs! In another minute he will be at the sill of the window. I will open the door and invite him in."

"No, no!" cried Grandfather weakly, jumping up from the chair and staring wildly about the room. "It will be the end of me."

"But think, Joseph, how my child will love it! He will splash and laugh—why, even now I can see him creeping under the door in his eagerness."

Without a word, gathering the baby Avril into his arms, Grandfather dashed out of the other door; and they watched him running across the fields and meadows, his white hair and beard flying back over his shoulders in the mad speed of his flight.

"Now there is a strange man," Grandmother said to Uncle Pablôt.

Pablôt only whistled softly and looked wise.

"One would think," continued Grandmother, "that he would be grateful for a nice trip on the back of my child. He will come to my way of thinking all in good time." She looked around her critically. "The fire!" she said. "How fiercely the fire is burning! It quite makes me boil with anger; I won't have it, I hate it!" and she ran upon it, scattering the embers with a great hissing sound. "There now!" turning again to Pablôt. "Do you think that the room is in readiness for my son? Shall I open the floodgates and let him in?"

"How about Anjou?" asked Uncle Pablôt.

"Anjou can ride in his basket."

"And Philippe?"

"The little cradle by the bed that Avril sleeps in—an excellent boat! Jump in, Philippe, run and jump in, for we are going to make a voyage. I—let me see—this tub will suit me nicely; I have a fondness for tubs; and you, Pablôt, can run along the bank. Into your basket, Anjou, *quick*! You look strangely unhappy, my pet. Are we all ready? *Enter, my son!*"

Grandmother unlatched the door facing on the river; it flew back against the wall with a crash. What happened next was very confused in the mind of the startled Philippe. There was a great, swishing roar as the water of the river, swollen to unheard-of heights by the hard rain, leaped and tumbled into the room in masses and billows of silver foam. Tightly he clutched the rail of the crib as his strange boat tossed and turned and ducked and pitched and bobbed and spun around and around in the currents and cross currents and boiling waves. At last, when the water in the room had reached the level of the water outside, and therefore had suddenly quieted, he dared to look about him. Uncle Pablôt had disappeared; Grandmother was calmly sitting in her tub with a rapturous smile on her old face. "So impulsive!" she remarked conversationally to Philippe. "My son, the River," she explained. "He is so very glad to see me. Did you notice how he jumped and romped when I let him in? It made me very proud! But we must not waste our time floating idly here; there is to be a very important reunion of my whole family." And with that they were caught in an eddying current and swept out of the door: Anjou, with tail as erect as a mast; Philippe, wide-eyed and silent in his cradle boat; and Grandmother in her wooden tub, pleased and proud, the happy tears streaming down her cheeks.

Once you get over being frightened, it is really great good fun, so Philippe found, to go racing along a swift-flowing river in a little boat that nods to each passing wave. They passed tall reeds and rushes that waved gracefully to them from the shore, weeping willow trees, their wands gray-green and crystal with rain, gently caressing the surface of the water, emerald fields patterned with yellow flowers shining wet, mallows by the River's edge, white with glowing hearts of deep pink, deep pink with hearts of white.

Sometimes swiftly, sometimes slowly, but always and ever onward, "Grandmother's Son" carried them on his strong back; now through lowlands, and now between high banks of dark chocolaty mud, where, from the black portals of burrows and tunnels, the bright eyes of water animals gazed at them in astonishment. Yes, it was thoroughly delightful, but it was puzzling to Philippe; there were many things that he did not understand. He decided that he would ask Grandmother, who was floating close to him in her wooden tub.

Grandmother in her wooden tub.

"Grandmother Marianne," he called to her, "why do you call the river your son?"

"Look at me, Philippe. Have I not changed?" asked Grandmother. "I am no longer Grandmother Marianne," she said, "I am Grandmother Rain!... Without me there would be no puddles, no pools, no lakes, no ponds, no rills and runs and rivulets, no brooks and streams, no waterfalls, no rivers—their lovely and happy voices would die from the land. They are all my children. And if it were not for my children, there would be no ocean."

"What is the ocean?" asked Philippe, who had never been to the seashore.

"That, my Philippe," said Grandmother Rain, "is where I was born, and where all my children return. It is a beautiful place! And how your uncle loves to play there—a decidedly worthy man, your uncle, though at times a trifle flighty."

They passed a grove of trees, their bright branches reaching out over the water.

"How fresh and strong they look," cried Grandmother Rain. "They are always glad to see me, I can assure you. Oh, I have strange adventures, Philippe. Sometimes I am buried in the soft, brown earth, and you would think that would be the end of me, now wouldn't you? But no! I creep back into the air through trunks of trees, through blades of grass and stalks of flowers, and through the shoots of young corn. I trickle through an endless maze of underground passages into deep wells, or until I find a place where I can come bubbling up to the surface. Every living thing needs me and every living thing loves me, except sometimes little boys kept in from play—eh?"

Philippe felt guilty, and was about to apologize when Grandmother Rain put him at rest. "That is not quite true. There are others," she said, "who do a good deal of complaining about me; they say that I am an old spoil-sport just because I try to make myself pleasant at their parties and picnics. But if I were to leave them forever——" she made an odd little gesture of despair. "Would you like me to sing you a song?" she asked unexpectedly. "It might serve to pass the time."

"Please," said Philippe, who was getting a bit tired of floating aimlessly and never arriving anywhere.

"Very well." And this is what she sang:

GRANDMOTHER RAIN'S SONG

"Pitapat, pitapat, drip, drip, drip—

Pitapat, pitapat, slip, slip, slip,

Over roofs and windows, over garden walls,

Over fields and meadows—the gray rain falls!

"I fall upon the countryside, upon the city square;

I tap the silk umbrellas that are opened everywhere;

I wash away the dirt and dust that cloud the flower's face;

I fall on royal palaces, and in the market place——

For no one is too regal, and no one is too low

To receive the crystal blessing that I scatter as I go.

I freshen up the thirsty world, and make it clean and green,

The grass grows tall, and flowers bloom wherever I have been.

Although I lie in gutters, and slip through hole and crack,
And sometimes have my little joke by running down your back,
I make small children happy, for on me they may float
Their shiny bright, their red and white, their little new toy boat.
So think not that because I fall like tears I may be sad:
The sparkle in each drop of me is proof that I am glad!

"Pitapat, pitapat, drip, drip, drip—
Pitapat, pita——

"Ah! *There* he comes!" cried Grandmother Rain excitedly, forgetting to finish her song.

"Who?" asked Philippe, curious, like most boys.

"Who indeed?" replied Grandmother. "Look up the shore. Now we will have some sport!"

Philippe did as he was told, and saw a small figure hurrying toward them at a great pace. As the figure drew nearer, he saw that it was Uncle Pablôt, running along the edge of the water and stirring it to frenzy.

"Hold tight!" warned Grandmother from her tub.

Philippe needed no warning, for as Uncle Pablôt drew opposite to them, waves broke the smooth surface of the river and tossed his little crib about like a cockle shell. He could see, as he was twisted about, that the rising waves were creeping over the edge of Grandmother Rain's tub and swamping it—it was sinking lower and lower. "Be careful, Grandmother!" he cried frantically.

"This is what I call delightful!" replied that remarkable woman, tipping her tub until the water ran in and filled it with a deep gurgle. As she sank into the river she clapped her hands, whereupon there was a blinding flash and a peal of sharp thunder. A bigger wave than the rest washed Philippe, cradle and all, upon the shore. He was too dazed to understand for some moments just what had happened, but at length he spied Grandmother, already at some distance, riding the waves and swimming strongly with the current.

"Now I shall be in high time for the reunion!" she called back to him, the growing space between them making her voice very faint.

Poor, dear Grandmother! Whatever would become of her? She would drown most surely. But perhaps Uncle Pablôt, who had raced on down the bank, could save her——But no! He was strolling back; he had given up. Philippe ran to meet his uncle with tears in his eyes.

"Hello! So there you are, safe and sound and high and dry, eh? You see, I veered about; I thought we might take a little stroll together," explained Uncle Pablôt airily.

"Save her!" pleaded Philippe tearfully.

"Who? Grandmother Rain? Be calm, my boy, she is quite in her element."

"But unless we do something, the river will carry her far away!"

"Which is exactly what she wishes. She will be back again, never worry. She makes these little trips to the ocean quite frequently. Look, Philippe, the sun is coming out! The sun and Grandmother Rain do not get along well together; he always hides as soon as she has made her appearance, and when she has gone, he goes about mopping up the whole countryside."

Uncle Pablôt's calmness gave Philippe some comfort. He was grown up, and therefore wise; perhaps he knew the meaning of these strange things. "Do they always disagree, Grandmother and the sun?" asked Philippe.

"Not always. Sometimes, though rarely, you may see them together, and then they hang a rainbow flag across the sky as a sign of their truce. But come! We have much land to cover, we must hurry a little more."

"Where are we going, Uncle Pablôt?"

"What a silly question! How am I to know? I go wherever it pleases me at the moment, sometimes for days in one direction, and at other times this way and that quicker than you can think. And please do not call me Uncle Pablôt; I am your Uncle Wind."

Philippe felt rebuked; he trotted silently beside the tall, lean fellow, thinking him a not very pleasant companion. He would gladly have walked home alone, but he had no idea where he was, and he was afraid to be left alone. At length his Uncle Wind spoke to him:

"Do not think unkindly of me, little Philippe. If I was cross to you, it is because I am given to complaining at times, but I am a good fellow at heart. With Grandmother Rain's help, I keep the world a nice clean place to live in. And do you know, Philippe, the best part of it is that I am such a humorous fellow; I am all the time playing the most amusing jokes! Why—once I mussed up the hair of a prince and ran off with the parasol of a duchess.... There now! I think I told you that once before, didn't I? But where and when it is quite past my ability to remember. Well, that gives you the idea. Hats? There is nothing quite so much fun as hats! Snatch a hat and run, drop it until its owner is just about to pick it up, and then snatch and run again. There's nothing that draws such a large and appreciative audience as the hat trick. Though, of course, umbrellas are great sport—but I need Grandmother Rain to help me with that trick. Maybe you think I am only a practical joker? Not at all! Do you remember that day you were sick, and your head felt as if it were on fire? Do you remember how I came and cooled it for you, and played with the tassels of the curtains until sundown to keep you amused? If I get a bit angry and rough at times, I am gentleness itself at others, and particularly am I loved in places that are hot and stuffy and saddened by ill health. I am one of the housekeepers of the earth, and I must be everlastingly at it to make things comfortable and shipshape. Oh! The dirt and the dust, the smoke and the foul smells people throw into my face in the cities, little dreaming that if it were not for me the earth would be unfit to live on. But I am strong without end and do my best. Yes, Philippe, I may bluster and blow and play tricks, but for all that I am a very excellent fellow. And I am a traveler and adventurer over land and sea, such as one has never read of in the most thrilling books! No one has seen more of the world than I. I have seen strange parts of the world, looked behind walls of ice, where no living thing has ever been. Only the other day——"

On and on talked Uncle Wind, and on and on traveled the two together. Over more meadows they went than Philippe thought could possibly be crowded into the world, and past innumerable herds of cows and flocks of sheep. It had grown warm with the coming of the sun, and often would workers in the fields spread wide their arms and speak words of welcome as they passed. The grass and the yellow wheat bowed as they stepped lightly over them and even the trees nodded in friendly recognition. Birds, stretching their wings, took rides on Uncle Wind's shoulders. At times Uncle Wind would go quite fast, so that Philippe had to run, and again, so slowly that they were scarcely creeping, until, after a long time, they stopped quite still on the top of a high hill.

"I often lie down and rest at sunset," explained Uncle Wind in a voice that was scarcely above a whisper.

Far, far away, Philippe saw, through a twilight haze of gold, what he had never seen before: the deep ocean where Grandmother Rain was holding her family reunion. The crimson sun was rolling over the blue edge of the world into its sparkling heart. He sat down in the crevice of a rock and thought long and wonderingly of the things that had come to pass that day, and he tried to see, in the land that was spread like a map before his eyes, the red roof and clump of trees that would be his own home. He did so long to be with his darling mother again! And very soon it would be dark.... Silver stars began to shine in a pale green sky.... Golden stars were lit in a sky of deepening purple.... More and more stars in a sky dark blue. Night had suddenly closed in around him, and he was frightened and started to cry.

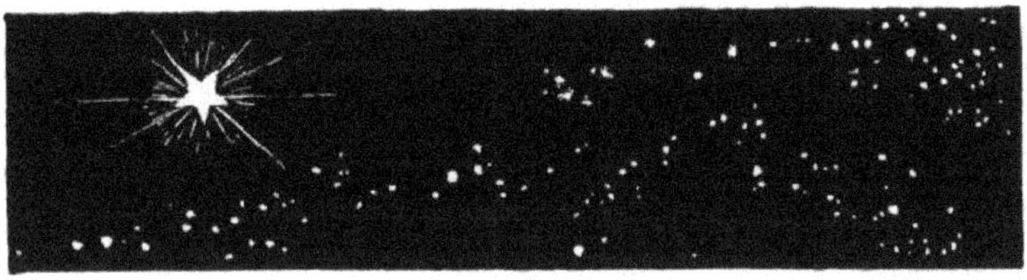

"Uncle Pablôt—I mean, Uncle Wind—I want to go home!"

But where was Uncle Wind? There was no answer, no sound, and search as carefully as he would, Philippe could find no trace of him. It was as if he had utterly vanished, which, indeed, he had, for the time being.

What was poor Philippe to do? The hilltop stones that surrounded him took menacing forms; he was sure that he saw the shining eyes, green and glowing, of prowling beasts. He summoned all his courage and bravely started to walk—where? Downhill, for he remembered that Grandmother Rain had told him, as they floated along the river, that that was the only way any sensible person would ever care to travel. Besides, when you were on the top of a hill, unless you stayed there, there was no other choice. Where else he was bound for he had no idea, but anything would be better than the unbroken stillness of the haunted rocks. How far he walked, at times ran, through the dark night, falling over roots and tearing his way through scratching brambles, pursued by unseen terrors of darkness, before he came to the old man, he had no idea.

At first he was timid of approaching the bent figure sitting huddled on a stump, so dim under the starlight. But loneliness and the longing for companionship overcame his fear.

"Please, sir," he said, drawing slowly closer, "please, sir, could you tell me—— *Grandfather Joseph! Grandfather Joseph!*"—and he flung his arms around Grandfather's neck, the hot tears streaming down his cheeks. But how cold Grandfather was! The touch of Grandfather's face against Philippe's burned like ice.

"Watch out!" said Grandfather sharply, "You are so insufferably warm you will melt me, if I do not succeed in freezing you first. And, young Philippe, be careful the names you call people. Look carefully at me again; do you not know me?"

Philippe was doubtful. Surely it was Grandfather Joseph, and yet—Grandfather had never been so cold, nor so strange in his behavior. Did he know him?

"Yes—no," answered Philippe, not being able to decide.

"Yes, *Snow*, that is right! I am Grandfather Snow."

"It's very upsetting!" remarked the puzzled boy.

"Is it?" replied Grandfather Snow coldly.

"But I may stay here with you, Grandfather? I was so frightened alone in the black night. I was out walking with Uncle Wind, and—and he seemed to disappear, and then I lost my way."

"You may stay if you do not come too close. So Uncle Wind vanished, did he? Your Uncle Wind is a fickle, changeable, unreliable fellow, but he has a will of his own and will turn up in time. I am very dependent on Uncle Wind; I can do nothing but lie around, without him."

"He is very nice, isn't he, Grandfather?" ventured Philippe.

"Aye, sometimes," replied the old man. "He was all gentleness this afternoon, but wait until you see him to-night! If I'm not mistaken in the signs, he will be in a fury. Then watch out for yourself, Young Impudence! When Uncle Wind is in a fury, he is a hard master and drives every one before him with a stinging lash. You'll see!"

Since Grandfather was in such a chilling mood, Philippe did not bother to talk with him, but sat at a little distance, thankful for companionship, and watched the winking of the stars, which, even as he watched them, sparkled and went out like sparks in the soot of a chimney, or as if a black curtain were being drawn across the black sky. After a long while, after the last star had vanished and the noiseless quiet of the night hemmed them in like an invisible wall, Grandfather Snow sprang to his feet and stood tensely listening with his hand to his ear.

"What is it, Grandfather?" Philippe asked, alarmed.

"Hush!... Hush!... Ah—now I hear it plainly!"

Philippe put his hand to his ear as he had seen Grandfather do, and listened intently, holding his breath that he should not miss the tiniest sound. Nothing. Yes—a far away and tiny sound. It sounded to Philippe like the little gasping noises he had made when he was learning to whistle, before ever he had been able to attempt a tune, the noise of air breathed in and out through rounded lips.

"*He is coming!*" Grandfather told him in a voice trembling with excitement. "And he is perfectly furious; seldom have I heard him whistle more beautifully. *Listen!*"

Philippe no longer had to strain to hear the far-away whistling; it was growing nearer every second, and as it approached it became high and shrill. "Is that my Uncle Wind making all that noise, Grandfather?"

"Aye!" said Grandfather shortly, crouching close to the ground in the position of a runner about to start a race.

"I shall run and meet him," cried Philippe, delighted at the idea of seeing his old friend again, who was now evidently very close. He had not run twelve steps when something spinning through the dark ran squarely into him, bowled him off his feet and rolled him along the ground as easily as if he had been made of thistledown. It was a terrific struggle he had to gain his feet again, and even when he had, and would have liked to stop to catch his breath and dust off the new suit his mother had made for him, he found himself being shoved roughly from behind.

"Faster! Faster! *Faster!*" screamed a voice in his very ears. And if he tried to slow up ever so little, "Rush! Rush! *Rush!*" the voice would command.

"Faster! faster! *faster!*"

"Please, Uncle Wind—oh, please, Uncle Wind—I can't go any faster—my legs aren't long enough!"

"*Faster!*" screamed Uncle Wind in anger, prodding poor Philippe so hard that he was fairly lifted off his feet.

Above them, and all around them, there was the noise of tearing leaves and crashing branches, there was the groaning of tortured trees as Uncle Wind lashed them with his invisible cat-o'-ninetails. Dim shadows streaked past like flying beasts. "Rush!" shrieked Uncle Wind, "R-U-SHSHSHshshshshsh——"

Something cold and stinging struck across Philippe's face, and it was then, in spite of his breathless panic at the mad flight, that he wanted to burst out laughing, for he saw that Grandfather, who had all this time been running at his side, was going so fast that he was actually losing his whiskers! "Your whiskers, Grandfather! The wind is tearing your whiskers off!" But the old man, who was speeding along more lightly than any rabbit, paid no attention. In truth, it seemed no great calamity, for as fast as Uncle Wind would tear off his whiskers and his hair and scatter them on the ground, new would grow immediately—and so thick and fast they grew that the ground became covered with white. But whiskers were not cold and wet when they brushed across one's face: they scratched and tickled, as Philippe had found out on occasions when he had kissed Grandfather. This was snow! Grandfather Snow was spreading his white blanket over the earth.

All night long Uncle Wind and Grandfather Snow sped across the dark country like mad men, and when little Philippe grew too tired to stand it any longer, Uncle Wind would lift him up in his strong arms and carry him. And the snow grew deep, and eddied and twisted into great mounds and high drifts with sharp, curved edges like the thin crests of waves—so that in the cold, pale light of the coming morning, the world looked like a beautiful dream cut from marble.

And with the coming of dawn, Uncle Wind suddenly stopped driving them.

"That was a great run!" said Uncle Wind. "It has left me completely out of puff. Philippe, my boy, I hope it hasn't tired you too much? Grandfather Snow, didn't I drive you beautifully?"

"Aye."

"And you have not done so badly. It will be some days before we are in shape for another run like that. Well, good-by! I think I shall do my famous vanishing act again. How about you, Grandfather?"

"Not quite yet. I shall linger on a bit. There are a few touches, a few light touches I neglected in my hurry last night that I would like to attend to this morning. You see," he explained to Philippe when Uncle Wind had vanished, "I am quite an artist. Some people think I am very little use and only good for lying around. Not at all! I make excellent snowballs, for one thing, and Uncle Wind is not the only member of our family who has knocked a hat off! But of course I would never tell you of such a thing if I did not know that you were too much of a gentleman to use me for such a purpose. No, no, my child, I work as hard for the things that grow, in my own way, as Grandmother Rain does in hers, but chiefly I delight to make things beautiful. See that naked gray tree? How bare and cold it looks! It needs a few high lights that I could not stop to give it last night—" whereupon Grandfather Snow touched each branch and twig with a powdering from his white beard, and the twig and branch of every tree around, until the whole world above the level of the ground was a tracery of gleaming, fairy lace. "Not bad, Philippe, not a bit bad! Can you see anything else that needs touching up? Speak out before it is too late, for my supply is nearly exhausted."

"Please, Grandfather, it is beautiful, but I am cold and tired, and I would like to go where it is warm."

"Of course you would, my child. Look! Below us in the valley it is green, and even from here one can see that there are flowers. Run on down——"

"I don't want to run; I'm tired of running!"

"Well, well," laughed Grandfather, "walk then, if you wish. After a while, when the warm sun comes to view my handiwork, I, too, will slip down into the valley, but I shall not stop there. No, I have a long way to travel before I join Grandmother Rain once more."

Philippe turned slowly away, touched by the purity and peace that surrounded him. "Good-by.... Good-by ..." said Grandfather Snow gently, very, very gently!

As Philippe reached the green valley below, the sun broke through a thin veil of silver clouds. It had risen brilliant and white from its all night dip into the distant ocean, and its cheering warmth was gratefully received by the tired adventurer. A fragrance, mingled of evergreens and flowers, herbs and damp earth, filled the motionless air, and from the end of the grass-grown lane, along which he walked lazily, there was an amazing confusion of sounds, as if thousands of birds were singing at one time. The lane led him to a gate, and on the gate was a sign which said:

PHILIPPE'S GARDEN

"I must have been away a long time for my garden to have grown so big," Philippe told himself.

Standing inside the gate was little Avril in a new green smock prettily embroidered with wreaths and garlands of flowers. She curtsied so low before him that the hem of her dress brushed the young shoots of grass; and she smiled at him tenderly.

"And who are you?" asked Philippe warily.

"Why, Philippe! Don't you know me?"

"Yes, I think I do; but I thought that I knew Grandmother Marianne and she turned out to be Grandmother Rain. Uncle Pablôt, it seems, was not Uncle Pablôt at all, but Uncle Wind. And my Grandfather Joseph is Grandfather Snow and lies just above us on the hill. It is very puzzling; can I be sure that you have not changed your name?"

"I have quite a number of names," explained the little girl. "Some call me Spring, some call me Flora, but you may call me Avril. Avril: April—it is all the same. Would you like me to show you your garden? It is very lovely, and I have worked hard to get it all in readiness for your coming."

"You?"

"Yes. I am your gardener, but I have had a lot of help. Every one has been so kind! Uncle Wind helped me plant it, Grandfather Snow prepared the ground in fine shape, and Grandmother Rain has been here often and often, giving my little plant babies their bottles. It has been a lot of worry and care, Philippe," Avril told him in a curiously grown-up voice, "but when you see my beautiful children, I am sure that you will think that it was worth while.

"Now here," she said, smiling happily and taking him by the hand, "are some of my first babies: the snowdrops, named in honor of their godfather, Grandfather Snow. And here——"

From flower to flower they wandered.

From bed to bed, from border to border they wandered, looking at the flowers, breathing the sweet perfume, and watching the clumsy but clever bees, out marketing for honey which they would pay for with golden pollen dust carried on their velvet backs. There were soft-petaled pansies as dark as midnight, as purple as a queen's dress, as yellow as the sun, and sometimes of many colors curiously combined to form impish and laughing faces. There were lilies of the valley and violets, stonecrop and candytuft, peonies and roses, larkspur and bridal wreath—so many flowers that Philippe could not remember their names, but gave himself up to the enjoyment of their soft and gorgeous colors, their delicate and magnificent shapes. Farther along the maze of paths where he was led by Avril, the flowers were still furled in tight buds, and at length they came to beds where the dark loam was scarcely more than broken by lifting sprouts. "These are for later," explained his fairylike guide.

"And these?" asked Philippe, when they had entered into a new part of the garden where straight rows of green-growing things were marked off in beds of checkerboard design.

"These funny little fellows," Avril told him, "are not as beautiful and proud as the flowers; they hold their heads less high, but they are all extremely worthy and one would find it difficult to get along without them."

"They look good enough to eat," said Philippe, who was beginning to feel very empty.

"They are," said Avril.

"And is all this garden mine?" asked Philippe.

"Yes," answered the little girl, curtsying again before him, and added: "All yours—King Philippe!"

"Oh, you mustn't call me 'King,' that is, when we're not playing games, you know," Philippe warned her, rather shocked. "Kings are grand people with treasures hidden away in strong chests, and they wear crowns of gold and have thousands of servants. I know, because I have read all about them in a book which my mother gave to me. I am a farmer's son, and can never be so wonderful a person as a King."

His companion looked at him very thoughtfully, and at last spoke:

"You are a King, Philippe. Sun, Moon, and Stars shine down upon your head a crown; the whole earth is yours, the great strong chest of hidden treasures. From the time the first small star hung like a lonely spark in space, your servants have been preparing for you a kingdom, the kingdom of Earth, than which there is only one greater. And that kingdom, too, will be yours some day if you rule wisely and well in this, and are kind, and strong-and gentle."

"It may be true," said Philippe, rather bewildered by the wonderful things he was hearing. "But I am quite sure that I have no servants; why—little though I am, even I must help my father in the fields."

"We are all your servants. Is it not true, Grandmother Rain?"

A shower suddenly passed over the garden, decking the flowers in crystal splendor, and from a small cloud overhead Philippe could distinctly hear the voice of Grandmother: "Yes. I have worked for Philippe's father and his grandfathers from the very beginning of things, and I hope to work for his children and his childrens' children for time evermore. Do not think badly of me, Philippe, if I do not come and go just to your liking, for I am very busy, with much important work to attend to."

"Is it not true, Grandfather Snow?"

"Aye, so it is!" came a voice from the bright hill beyond the garden wall.

"Is it not true, Uncle Wind?"

"Well, well! I am just in time," remarked Uncle Wind, sauntering up the garden path, the flowers nodding to him as he passed. He had cast aside his great cloak, but even then looked a little warm. "Just wandered up from the Southlands," he continued. "Yes, my little darling, it is true enough what you are telling Philippe, but of course we are not to be bossed about like ordinary servants; we serve and yet we keep our independence; we have been at our various tasks so long that we know exactly what to do without being told, and if we seem a little lazy at times, or a little too enthusiastic at others, remember that we may have our own very good reasons. Yes, indeed," he went on, commencing to bluster a bit, "there are often reasons hidden in the strangest things we do. Did I ever tell you how once I mussed up the hair of a prince and ran off with the parasol of a duchess——"

"The wind is capable of being a little monotonous at times," Avril whispered into Philippe's ear, but he could hardly hear her, for the garden was being filled with other voices, coming from here, there, and everywhere—from the grass, and the flowers, and the vegetables, and the trees, from the stones, and even from the brown earth itself, and they all were saying in their own way, the one thing: "We serve!"

"Please listen to us a moment," pleaded the fragile voices of the flowers. "We serve too, though many consider us too delicate and concerned about our own looks to be of much use. But do not forget us, Philippe! Do not forget us when you are grown up and your mind is crowded with worries and cares and a lot of things that will seem more important to you than they really are. Keep a place for us in your mind and heart, and we will repay you in our mysterious way a hundredfold and more. Do as we ask; treasure beauty, purity, and truth—for though you may love us now, you will not understand the full importance of our message until you have grown up. Do not forget——"

"The flowers are very talkative to-day," remarked one little lettuce to another.

"The flattery of the bees has quite turned their heads," agreed a radish who was notably sharp, whereupon some of the more sensitive flowers who had overheard blushed deeply.

But Philippe heard none of this chatter of the vegetables, for it seemed that the whole world, the ox and the ass, the horse and the cow, the tame beasts of the fields and the wild beasts of the spaces beyond, the fox and the rabbit, the mouse and the beetle, the creatures that crawled and the creatures that ran, the cricket and the grasshopper and the inhabitants of air and ocean, the little hills and high hills, the valleys and forests, the voice of water through the land, sky and earth—all, *all* were joining in a great, droning chant: "We serve—we serve—we serve——"

"What utter nonsense!" shouted a little bird saucily, flying from the low branches of a tulip tree. "I serve no one; I just have lots of fun, and I'm going to have an exciting fly—and that's something little boys can't do, for they haven't even any pin feathers!"

The cocky way the little bird flapped her wings and tossed her head made Philippe double up with laughter.

"See!" said the little rebel's mate, flying close. "You have made the King laugh, so your empty boasting has broken like a bubble, for laughter is one of the greatest services in the world! And as for going on your wild flight, have you forgotten our pretty blue eggs in their soft brown nest?"

"I am a King!" said Philippe in a daze of wonderment. "My darling Avril, tell me what I can do to show my gratitude to all my servants."

"They love nothing better than that you use them, Philippe. Use them wisely and well, and not only for yourself—but for others." And gentle Spring kissed him upon the lips, filling his heart with love and happiness.

"It is high time," said Philippe's mother to Philippe's father, "that our little one was back. Soon it will be dark."

She went to the doorway and gazed across the fields.

"Here comes Pablôt," she called back into the room, "and he is carrying the child in his arms."

"Sh-h-h-h-h!" breathed Uncle Pablôt, drawing close. "Take your son gently into your arms; he has been sleeping bravely all the way from his grandparents'. And here," said Uncle Pablôt, "is his little silver whistle, by which I hope that he will remember me when he wakes up and finds me gone."

CPSIA information can be obtained
at www.ICGtesting.com
Printed in the USA
LVHW052357021121
702257LV00007B/828

9 789355 343086